TINLEY PARK PUBLIC LIBRARY
7851 TIMBER DRIVE
TINLEY PARK, IL 60477
708-532-0160 / FAX 708-532-2981

summer
COOKING

summer
COOKING

KITCHEN-TESTED RECIPES FOR
Picnics • Patios • Grilling
AND MORE

Chicago Tribune

S
SURREY
BOOKS

AN AGATE IMPRINT

CHICAGO

Printed in China

Summer Cooking
First printing February 2015
Hard cover
ISBN-13: 978-1-57284-171-0
ISBN-10: 1-57284-171-0

Chicago Tribune
Tony W. Hunter, CEO & Publisher
Gerould W Kern, Senior Vice President, Editor
Joyce Winnecke, President, Tribune Content Agency
Peter Kendall, Managing Editor
Colin McMahon, Associate Editor
George Papajohn, Investigations Editor
Margaret Holt, Standards Editor
R. Bruce Dold, Editorial Page Editor
John P. McCormick, Deputy Editorial Page Editor
Marcia Lythcott, Commentary Editor
Amy Carr, Development Editor
Associate Managing Editors
   Geoff Brown, Entertainment
   Robin Daughtridge, Photography
   Mike Kellams, Business
   Joe Knowles, Sports

Library of Congress Cataloging-in-Publication Data has been applied for.

10 9 8 7 6 5 4 3 2 1

Surrey Books is an imprint of Agate Publishing. Agate books are available in bulk at discount prices. For more information visit agatepublishing.com.

about this book

"Summer Cooking" contains the very best summertime recipes from the Chicago Tribune's legendary test kitchen. For this book, the Tribune selected dishes and beverages that took advantage of the freshest and most delicious seasonal ingredients and emphasized simplicity for those hot summer days when the last thing you'll want to do is spend hours in a hot kitchen. Whether you're enjoying these delights on your patio, straight from a picnic basket in Millennium Park or around your dining table, you'll love the recipes just as much as we do.

contents

summer quenchers
DRINKS FOR A THIRSTY CREW **PAGE 9**

for starters
WARM-WEATHER APPETIZERS **PAGE 43**

refreshing eats
SIDE AND ENTREE SALADS **PAGE 69**

handfuls
EASY-TO-PACK MAIN DISHES **PAGE 121**

summer's best main dishes
GRILLED AND SLOW-COOKED DELIGHTS **PAGE 147**

cool treats
DESSERTS **PAGE 191**

credits
ARTICLE AND RECIPE CREDITS **PAGE 205**
PHOTO CREDITS **PAGE 210**

index
PAGE 213

summer quenchers

DRINKS FOR A THIRSTY CREW

FAMILY-FRIENDLY NONALCOHOLIC DRINKS

basic backyard lemonade p. 10
fruit smoothie p. 13
lemon balm iced tea p. 15

ADULT BEVERAGES: ALCOHOLIC DRINKS

caipirinha p. 16
« mojito p. 18
batida p. 19
the mambo p. 20
pisco sour p. 21
chocolate-covered grasshopper p. 22
raspberry-lemon slam p. 24
daiquiri p. 25
homemade limoncello p. 26
sorrento sunset p. 28
nevisian smile p. 29
red sangria p. 31
le jardin de huguenots p. 32
mango, plum and peach sangria p. 33
amere p. 35
bella fragola p. 36
house G+T p. 40

basic backyard lemonade

makes 2½ cups
prep: 5 minutes

THERE'S SOMETHING ENDEARING ABOUT LEMONADE. FOR MANY OF US, IT WAS the first tart or sweet-sour beverage we tasted. It very well may have been the first recipe we made in the kitchen (with Mom's help). It might also have given us our first taste of the world of commerce. Happily, kids still sell lemonade from jury-rigged sales counters in front of their homes. The smell and taste of the lemon's juice and zest are as provocative and evocative as ever.

½ cup freshly squeezed lemon juice	2 cups cold water
¼ cup superfine sugar	2 or 3 ice cubes per glass

① Combine lemon juice and sugar; stir until sugar dissolves. Add cold water; stir again.

② Pour over ice in tall glasses; serve with a straw, if desired.

fruit smoothie

serves 2

prep: 5 minutes

THE 150 TO 400 CALORIES IN A NUTRIENT-DENSE SMOOTHIE CAN MAKE A significant difference in evening workouts (or even night-time business meetings). Research shows athletes who get adequate nutrition in the four hours before exercise will be 20 percent stronger during the last 10 minutes of a game or practice than competitors who didn't get enough good food. This low-fat, high-carbohydrate drink was developed in the Tribune test kitchen.

6 ice cubes

1 banana

1 kiwi

¾ cup guava nectar or any fruit juice

½ cup non-fat soy milk

½ cup each, fresh or frozen: blueberries, strawberries

1 Blend all ingredients in blender until smooth.

lemon balm iced tea

serves 2
prep: 10 minutes

THIS RECIPE, ADAPTED FROM CHEF DAVID BURNS OF THE FORMER LE MERIDIEN Chicago, uses the citrus-mint hit of lemon balm. But any mint—spearmint, peppermint or a flavored mint such as chocolate—could be substituted.

2 cups each: ice, unsweetened iced tea

2 tablespoons lemon balm simple syrup, recipe follows

6 sprigs fresh lemon balm

Juice of 1 lemon

① Combine ice, iced tea, simple syrup, 4 sprigs of the lemon balm and lemon juice in a container; cover and shake well. Pour into ice-filled glasses. Garnish each glass with sprig of lemon balm and wedge of lemon, if desired.

---

herb-flavored simple syrups

makes 1½ cups
prep: 15 minutes / cook: 5 minutes / stand: 30 minutes

SIMPLE SYRUPS ARE APTLY NAMED: ALL YOU DO IS DISSOLVE SUGAR INTO WAter on the stovetop for an incredible burst of flavor. Use these to sweeten iced teas and sparkling waters as well as cocktails and sparkling wine. Simple syrups will keep up to three months in an airtight container in the refrigerator.

1 cup sugar

¾ cup water

Choice of herb (we recommend lavender, lemon balm, mint, rosemary, sage or basil)

① Combine the sugar and water in a small saucepan; heat to a boil over medium-high heat. Add the herbs, pushing them under the surface with a spoon; remove the saucepan from the heat. Cover; let herbs steep 30 minutes.

② Pour syrup through a sieve, pressing firmly on herbs with the back of a spoon to extract all of the syrup. Discard herbs.

caipirinha

makes 1 drink
prep: 10 minutes

SAVVY CHICAGO SIPPERS KNOW THE DIFFERENCE BETWEEN MARGARITAS AND mojitos. They can debate the merits of a well-made pisco sour. And, without hesitation, they will ask bartenders for a caipirinha (that's ky-ee-pea-REEN-hya) without missing a beat. Is it the citrus-liquor marriage that makes these drinks naturals on sultry summer days? Do we simply love the flavors of cachaca (KAH-sha-sa), the distilled-from-sugar-cane-juice liquor from Brazil? This cocktail is adapted from a recipe by Nacional 27 restaurant.

Rose's lime juice

Granulated sugar

1 lime, cut in wedges

¼ cup lime simple syrup, recipe follows

¼ cup cachaca

① Moisten rim of tall tumbler with lime juice; dip rim in sugar.

② Add lime wedges and syrup to glass. Press limes, using muddler or pestle, to release juice and oils in skin.

③ Add cachaca. Fill glass with crushed ice. Stir.

simple syrup

makes 1 cup

prep: 5 minutes / cook: 10 minutes / chill: at least 1 hour

¾ cup each: sugar, water

① Heat sugar and water in small, heavy saucepan over medium heat. Cook, stirring occasionally, until sugar is completely dissolved, about 10 minutes.

② Cover; refrigerate until chilled, at least 1 hour.

NOTE: Any remaining simple syrup can be refrigerated for up to several weeks.

VARIATIONS

☛ TO MAKE LIME SYRUP, add zest of 2 limes to warm syrup. Refrigerate zest in syrup until ready to use; strain.

☛ TO MAKE MINT SYRUP, substitute mint leaves for zest.

mojito

makes 1 drink
prep: 10 minutes
pictured on p. 8

ACHANGE OF PACE IS GOOD, ESPECIALLY WHEN THE PACE FROM WHICH YOU seek a change is frantic. So when you are invited to a tropical landscape far, far away, you accept, frantically. Behold, the tranquilizing effects of the hand-muddled mojito.

3 slices lime, scrubbed

6 fresh mint leaves

2 teaspoons sugar

½ cup crushed ice

1½ ounces (3 tablespoons) rum (Bacardi Limon recommended)

Splash (roughly 2 tablespoons) club soda

① Settle the lime, mint leaves and sugar in the bottom of a sturdy 6-ounce glass. Muddle, which is to say mash, until limes have released their juice and mint leaves are looking tattered. A muddler—wooden pestle—would be the classic tool. But a fork also works.

② Scoop the ice into the glass. Cover and shake.

③ Add the rum. Top with the soda. No need for a sprig of mint or a slice of lime garnish. The mojito is a refreshing delight, not a looker.

batida

makes 1 drink
prep: 5 minutes

A T RESTAURANTS AND SNACK SHOPS, GLASS BARRELS OF TART-SWEET aguas frescas (roughly translated as "cool waters") come in pineapple, watermelon, hibiscus and mango flavors, among others. Restaurants keep their electric blenders whirring with batidos and their culinary cousin, licuados (lee-KWA-dose). Drink masters suggest using one juice or blending your own mix in this batida.

Confectioners' sugar	¼ cup fruit juice concentrate: mango, guava or passion fruit
Ice cubes	Lime slice
3 tablespoons cachaca	
1 to 2 tablespoons bar or simple syrup, see recipe on p. 17	

① Dip rim of short tumbler or old-fashioned glass in confectioners' sugar.

② Fill shaker with ice. Add cachaca, syrup and fruit juice concentrate. Shake well. Strain into glass over ice. Garnish with lime slice.

the mambo

makes 1 drink
prep: 5 minutes

R um, that liquor made from sugar cane juice or molasses, sweetens this delicious drink. Adapted from a recipe by the former Mambo Grill.

⅓ cup each: fresh orange juice, pineapple juice

¼ cup fresh lime juice

2 tablespoons light rum

1 tablespoon 151-proof rum

Ice cubes

Orange twist, maraschino cherries

① Stir together juices and rums in pitcher. Pour into highball glass filled with ice cubes. Garnish with orange twist and cherries.

pisco sour

makes 1 drink
prep: 5 minutes

THE MADE-FROM-GRAPES AGED BRANDY CALLED PISCO MAKES THIS DRINK truly unique.

½ cup ice

3 tablespoons pisco brandy

2 tablespoons fresh lime juice

1 tablespoon sugar

½ egg white, optional

Ground cinnamon, optional

Lime wedge

① Puree all ingredients, except cinnamon, in blender. Pour into glass. Sprinkle top with cinnamon; garnish with lime wedge.

chocolate-covered grasshopper

makes 4 six-ounce cocktails
prep: 6 minutes / cook: 1 minute

VANILLA ICE CREAM'S SOCIABILITY MAKES IT A GREAT MIXER IN MANY FROZEN cocktails. Our version of the venerable grasshopper uses a chocolate mint sauce that freezes after you drizzle it over the frozen drink.

½ cup (about 3 ounces) soft chocolate mint candies, such as Junior Mints, plus additional candies for garnish

1 tablespoon butter

2 cups plus 1 tablespoon vanilla ice cream

¼ cup plus 2 tablespoons green creme de menthe

¼ cup white creme de cacao

10 ice cubes

① Put ½ cup of the candy, butter and 1 tablespoon of the ice cream in microwave-safe bowl; microwave on high until heated through, about 1 minute. Stir until mixture thickens to consistency of a sauce. Set aside.

② Combine 2 cups of the ice cream, creme de menthe, creme de cacao and ice cubes in blender; blend until drink is thick and creamy, about 1 minute. Pour mixture into 4 martini glasses; drizzle chocolate sauce over drink. Garnish with cocktail skewers of candies, if desired.

raspberry-lemon slam

serves 6
prep: 5 minutes

Fresh berries and lemon liven up this tequila cocktail. You'll find that it's great for a crowd of any size on a summer day.

1 cup each: frozen unsweetened raspberries, orange liqueur, Grand Marnier preferred

¾ cup blanco tequila

½ cup fresh lemon juice

2 tablespoons superfine sugar
Ice cubes

6 thin slices lemon

① Combine berries, liqueur, tequila, lemon juice, sugar and 8 ice cubes in blender container. Blend until smooth.

② Fill 6 highball glasses with ice cubes; pour mixture over them. Garnish each glass with a lemon slice.

daiquiri

makes 1 drink

prep: 5 minutes

THE DAIQUIRI, LIKE THE MOJITO, SHARES CUBAN HERITAGE. COCKTAIL HISTORY claims it was named for Cuba's Daiquiri Beach (or village or iron mine) and mastered at El Floridita Bar in Havana.

Crushed ice (enough to half fill a cocktail shaker)

1½ ounces (3 tablespoons) rum

1 tablespoon lime juice

1 tablespoon powdered sugar

1 slice lime

① Half fill a cocktail shaker with ice. Add the rum, lime juice and sugar. Shake well.

② Pour into a cocktail glass. Garnish with a slice of lime.

homemade limoncello

makes 2½ quarts
prep: 30 minutes / macerate: 80 days

THIS RECIPE IS ADAPTED FROM ONE BY TOM BECKMAN, AN INSTRUCTOR AT THE Cooking and Hospitality Institute of Chicago (now Le Cordon Bleu College of Culinary Arts). Beckman said, "Limoncello always seemed awfully sweet to me. I wanted to back off on the sugar. Even as a pastry chef, I like stuff to really taste like what it is." He uses a vegetable peeler to remove the peel from the lemons while avoiding the pith. "It's so easy, anybody could do it. Only, it takes the patience to not open it up and drink it [before it's done]," Beckman said.

11 lemons
1 bottle (1.75 liters) vodka

3 cups simple syrup, see note

① Cut zest off lemons, taking care to cut off any of the white pith; reserve fruit for another use. Place peels and vodka in large glass jar or bottle with wide mouth. Seal top; place in dark, cool place 40 days. Swirl contents occasionally.

② Add simple syrup. Seal; let macerate 40 days. Remove peels when soaking time is up.

NOTE: To make simple syrup, combine 1½ cups sugar and 1½ cups water in saucepan. Cook over low heat until clear; raise heat to a boil for a minute. Cool before using.

sorrento sunset

makes 1 cocktail
prep: 5 minutes

THE ITALIAN VILLAGE RESTAURANTS FEATURE LIMONCELLO IN THIS COCKTAIL that combines the sweetness of the liqueur with the bitterness of Campari.

3 tablespoons limoncello, chilled

1½ tablespoons Campari

2 tablespoons fresh orange juice

Splash of soda water

1 each: orange slice, maraschino cherry

① In a Collins glass filled with ice, pour in limoncello, Campari and orange juice; finish with a splash of soda water. Garnish with a slice of orange folded around a cherry (called a flag) and held with a pick.

nevisian smile

makes 1 cocktail
prep: 10 minutes

From Nevis island in the Caribbean comes the wonderfully named "Nevisian smile" (rum, Irish cream liqueur, coffee-flavored liqueur, pineapple juice, coconut cream and coconut milk). Former beverage manager Paul Saliba of the Ritz-Carlton Chicago used this recipe from the Four Seasons Resort, Nevis.

- 6 tablespoons pineapple juice
- 3 tablespoons each: coconut cream, coconut milk
- 2 tablespoons each: rum, Irish cream liqueur, coffee liqueur
- 1 fresh pineapple slice, optional

① Crush two or three ice cubes in a blender. Combine all ingredients; blend until thick. Pour into a large snifter or hurricane glass; garnish with a slice of pineapple.

red sangria

serves 10
prep: 25 minutes

SANGRIA IS MORE THAN JUST A DRINK TO FABIAN PADILLA OF CHICAGO. HIS mother is from the Dominican Republic and his father from Puerto Rico, so sangria was a must-pour at any family gathering. "When I first started making it, sangria was a cultural thing," said Padilla, a Peterson Park resident. "Now sangria is hip."

3 ripe dark plums, halved, pitted	1 quart fruit punch
2 oranges, peeled	1½ cups lemon-lime soda
1 each, halved, cored: apple, pear	1 cup apple brandy
1 bottle (750 milliliters) shiraz	

① Cut the fruit into small pieces; place in a large pitcher or punch bowl. Add remaining ingredients; mix. Chill until ready to serve.

le jardin des huguenots

serves 10 to 12

prep: 20 minutes / macerate: 4–6 hours / chill: overnight

RODERICK HALE WEAVER AT HUSK RESTAURANT IN CHARLESTON, S.C., SAYS this punch was "inspired by the Huguenot settlers who were here in Charleston. ... It ended up tasting like a sangria, but a French version of sangria." He uses Jouclary, a soft red wine from the Languedoc-Roussillon region in France. Another soft red wine can sub.

Zest of 3 grapefruit

¾ cup demerara sugar (a raw sugar)

3 ounces fresh lemon juice, about 2 lemons

1½ ounces fresh orange juice, about 1 orange

½ bottle (1½ cups plus 2 tablespoons) Lillet Blanc

2 ounces Chartreuse

1 bottle (750 milliliters) soft red wine

Soda water

1 blood orange, sliced into very thin wedges

① Place grapefruit zest in a nonreactive container; sprinkle with sugar. Refrigerate, 4–6 hours.

② Add lemon and orange juices. Muddle, then stir until sugar is dissolved. Add Lillet, Chartreuse and red wine. Strain; chill overnight. To serve, add 1 ounce soda water to each 3-ounce portion of the red wine mixture. Serve with a large ice cube. Garnish with thin slices of blood orange.

mango, plum and peach sangria

serves 12
prep: 20 minutes

THIS RECIPE WAS CREATED BY FABIAN PADILLA OF CHICAGO. HE LIKES TO USE gewurztraminer, a slightly sweet but spicy white wine from Germany, in this sangria. Riesling is another option. Sprite is Padilla's preferred lemon-lime soda. Mango nectar is available at Hispanic markets, specialty markets and many supermarkets.

3 mangoes, peeled, pitted

2 red plums, halved, pitted

1 white peach, halved, pitted

1 bottle (750 milliliters) gewurztraminer

1 quart orange juice

1 can (12 ounces) mango nectar

2 cups lemon-lime soda

1 to 2 cups plain vodka or rum

① Chop fruits into bite-size pieces; place in a tall pitcher or punch bowl. Add remaining ingredients; mix. Chill until ready to serve.

house G+T (p. 40)

house G+T

makes 1 cocktail
prep: 5 minutes
pictured on pp. 38–39

HOT NIGHTS OFTEN CALL FOR NOT MUCH MORE THAN ICY LIQUID REFRESHMENT. This recipe by John Douglass, bar manager at Table, Donkey and Stick, replaces lime with grapefruit to create a more thirst-quenching drink. "It remains a bitter cocktail, but by using grapefruit I'm able to smooth it out," he says. Douglass uses Chicago's own Letherbee Original Label Gin, fresh-squeezed grapefruit juice and tonic syrup made with lemongrass, grapefruit rind, citric acid, kosher salt and cinchona bark, which provides that distinctive touch of quinine flavor. Citric acid and cinchona bark may be found at some supermarkets, health stores or online.

¾ **ounce tonic syrup, see recipe**

1½ **ounces gin**

Sparkling water

One-quarter grapefruit wheel

① Pack a double old-fashioned glass with ice cubes. Add tonic syrup and gin. Top with sparking water. Stir gently. Garnish with grapefruit quarter.

tonic syrup

makes 1 liter

prep: 20 minutes / cook: 25 minutes / stand: at least 1 hour / strain: 20 minutes

3 grapefruits

1 liter filtered water

3 cups cane sugar

2 stalks lemongrass, chopped

6 tablespoons citric acid

2 tablespoons cinchona bark powder

Kosher salt

① Cut the zest of 3 grapefruit into strips. Juice the grapefruit; reserve juice.

② Pour filtered water and cane sugar into a large stainless steel saucepan. Heat to boil. Immediately reduce heat to low and add grapefruit zest, lemongrass, citric acid, cinchona bark powder and 2 big pinches kosher salt. Stir. Cover; simmer 20 minutes.

③ Pass syrup through a strainer into a heat-proof container. Discard the solids; allow mixture to cool to room temperature, at least 1 hour.

④ Slowly stir in the reserved grapefruit juice. Strain the syrup again, this time through a coffee filter. For best results, do this in several batches using several coffee filters.

⑤ Bottle the syrup and refrigerate. Can be kept in refrigerator about a month.

for starters

WARM-WEATHER APPETIZERS

smoked salmon mousse p. 44

snappy sausage and cucumber rounds with mustard p. 47

wonton chicken bites p. 48

simple ceviche p. 51

nut stuffing for vegetables p. 52

shrimp on pesto rounds p. 53

olive-avocado dim sum p. 54

asian summer rolls p. 57

creamy basil-onion dip p. 58

vegetable-stuffed deviled eggs p. 60

cheese and rye cocktail sandwiches p. 61

mexican pinwheels p. 62

« chilled white gazpacho p. 63

pecorino crisp p. 64

prosciutto wrapped figs p. 67

smoked salmon mousse

makes 96 canapes
prep: 35 minutes / chill: 8 hours

SMOKED SALMON IS A DECIDEDLY GENEROUS (AND EXPENSIVE) WAY TO present an entire side of salmon, especially if it is sliced to order. But a terrine requires less salmon and little or no garnish and can be cut into small or large pieces depending on the number of guests. Make the terrine a day ahead or on the morning of the party. Instead of treating the loaf as a spread, unmold it and cut the loaf into pieces to fit atop crisp crackers or toasted bread cut into triangles or squares. Serve them garnished with chopped dill on a tray or plate.

1 pound smoked salmon, whole or pre-sliced, cut into large pieces

⅓ cup Bloody Mary mix

2 tablespoons fresh lemon juice

1 tablespoon vodka

¼ teaspoon salt or more, depending on saltiness of the salmon

⅛ teaspoon or more to taste each: ground black pepper, ground red pepper

2 envelopes (¼ ounce each) unflavored powdered gelatin

⅓ cup cold water

2 cups chilled whipping cream

Chopped dill or dill sprigs

① Place salmon in a food processor fitted with the metal blade; pulse until finely chopped. Add Bloody Mary mix, lemon juice, vodka, salt and peppers. Process to a smooth puree. Transfer to a large bowl; set aside.

② Combine gelatin and cold water in a custard cup. Let soak until gelatin is translucent, about 3 minutes. Heat in a microwave oven at 50 percent power until melted but not hot, about 40 seconds.

③ Meanwhile, pour cream into bowl of an electric mixer; beat on medium speed until soft peaks form. Turn mixer to low speed; slowly add liquid gelatin. Stop machine; add salmon puree. Mix on lowest speed until thoroughly blended and evenly colored.

④ Transfer salmon mixture to oiled 8-by-4-inch loaf pan, filling the mold evenly and smoothing top with a rubber spatula. Cover pan with plastic wrap; refrigerate at least 8 hours.

⑤ Unmold the terrine from the pan onto a cutting board. Cut crosswise into ½-inch-thick slices. Cut each slice into 6 pieces. Place on crackers; sprinkle with dill. Serve on a plate or platter.

snappy sausage and cucumber rounds with mustard

makes about 50 rounds
prep: 30 minutes / cook: 3 minutes

THE ARRAY OF SAUSAGES AT THE SUPERMARKET HAS GROWN DRAMATICALLY IN the last few years. Favorites include a smoked duck sausage with sun-dried tomatoes and artichokes and a chicken-apple sausage. For a quick party dish, you can stack cooked sausage slices on cucumber slices, and add some flavored mustard and pieces of roasted red pepper. It makes an attractive hors d'oeuvre with plenty of flavor. The mustard, as well as the sausage, can be varied. Use Creole mustard for a bite, or tarragon or dill mustards for an herbal flavor.

6 ounces smoked duck, chicken, turkey or other cooked sausage links, sliced ¼-inch thick

2 cucumbers, sliced ¼-inch thick

Creole or other flavored mustard

2 bottled, roasted red peppers, chopped or cut into thin strips

① Heat broiler. Place sausage slices on a baking sheet; spread tops with mustard. Broil until lightly browned, about 3 minutes; set aside.

② Spread cucumber slices on a cutting board. Top with a sausage slice, mustard side down. Drizzle a little more mustard on top of each slice. Top each with pieces of red pepper. Place on a serving platter.

wonton chicken bites

makes 36 pieces
prep: 10 minutes / cook: 8 minutes

INEXPENSIVE WONTON WRAPPERS ARE GREAT TO KEEP ON HAND FOR SPUR-OF-the-moment entertaining. The wrappers, traditionally used to prepare steamed, fried and boiled Chinese dumplings, also bake into tiny, attractive pastry cups with a slightly nutlike flavor in just 8 minutes. It's fun to experiment with fillings for the cups. Spoon in shrimp drizzled with cocktail sauce, roasted red pepper spread, crab dip and tuna pate. This Chinese chicken salad made with bottled sauces, a bag of shredded cabbage coleslaw and a roasted chicken from the deli is great when you have just enough time to rush through the express lane before guests arrive. Before pressing the dough into pastry cups, cut off a ½-inch strip to make the cups truly bite-size. Seal unbaked leftover wrappers in plastic wrap to reuse during the holiday season. Or, bake more wrappers than you plan to use at one time. They're surprisingly sturdy and travel well, unstuffed in a plastic bag. You can successfully store them up to three days without noticing a loss in crispness and flavor.

36 wonton wrappers

½ of a 16-ounce bag coleslaw

1 cup cooked, chopped chicken

1 can (8 ounces) water chestnuts, finely chopped

5 green onions, thinly sliced

2 teaspoons roasted sesame oil

4 tablespoons Chinese plum sauce

① Heat oven to 350 degrees. Cut a ½-inch strip off one side of each wonton skin; pleat wrappers into oiled mini-muffin tins to make cups. Bake until golden, 8 minutes. Let stand at least 5 minutes.

② Place cabbage, chicken, water chestnuts and green onions in a large bowl. Stir in sesame oil and plum sauce. Spoon into cooled wonton cups.

simple ceviche

serves 8

prep: 15 minutes / marinate: 1 hour

CEVICHE MAKES AN EXCELLENT WARM-WEATHER APPETIZER OR LIGHT LUNCH with crisp flavors that explode on the tongue. It can be made in minutes, and because for the most part it contains nothing but fresh fish, citrus juice and vegetables, it's very good for you.

- 1 pound firm fish like tilapia, salmon, cod or other very fresh fish, cut into ½-inch dice
- 4 garlic cloves, minced
- 1 jalapeno pepper, minced, or hot sauce to taste
- ½ cup freshly squeezed lime juice
- ¼ cup diced red onion
- 1 tablespoon minced cilantro
- ½ teaspoon salt
  Freshly ground pepper to taste
- 1 avocado, cut into ¾-inch dice, optional
- 1 ripe tomato, cut into ¾-inch dice, optional

① Combine all ingredients in a nonreactive bowl; marinate 1 hour in refrigerator. Serve with saltine crackers or tortilla chips.

nut stuffing for vegetables

makes 2½ cups
prep: 35 minutes / soak: 2 hours

RAW! IT'S A POWERFUL WORD IN THE WORLD OF FOOD. WHEN APPLIED TO DINing, it sets off strong emotions and evokes images of sparsely garnished plates, overly crunchy vegetables and minimal seasoning. But it doesn't have to be that way. This recipe, adapted from a recipe by raw food entrepreneur Karyn Calabrese, makes a tasty stuffing for mushrooms, celery, zucchini or cucumber boats. Look for hemp oil and spirulina flakes at health food stores.

1 cup each: sun-dried tomatoes, blanched almonds, pecan halves

1 avocado, peeled, pitted

2 cloves garlic, chopped

2 tablespoons hemp oil, pumpkin seed oil or olive oil

1 teaspoon coarse salt

Spirulina flakes to taste, optional

① Cover sun-dried tomatoes with warm water; soak until very soft, about 2 hours. Combine almonds and pecans in a large bowl and cover with warm water; let stand until swollen, about 30 minutes.

② Drain tomatoes and nuts. Combine tomatoes, nuts, avocado, garlic, oil and salt in the bowl of a food processor. Pulse 3 times; process until a semi-smooth paste forms, scraping bowl occasionally, about 5 minutes.

③ Transfer paste to a bowl; refrigerate until ready to fill vegetables. Sprinkle with spirulina flakes before serving.

shrimp on pesto rounds

makes 2 dozen pieces
prep: 25 minutes / cook: 1 minute

CALCULATING THE NUMBER OF HORS D'OEUVRES NEEDED CAN BE REDUCED TO a formula: Multiply the number of guests times the number of hors d'oeuvres they're likely to consume, then multiply that by the number of hours the event will last. Variables include how hungry the guests are likely to be, if the event is before or after a main meal, if the ratio of men to women is greater and if alcohol will be served. To save last-minute preparation time, purchase cooked shrimp or grill them the day before.

¼ cup mayonnaise

1½ tablespoons bottled or refrigerated pesto sauce

2 teaspoons chopped fresh basil

1 to 2 tablespoons olive oil

24 slices slender (about 1½ inches in diameter) French bread

½ each, cut into fine julienne: yellow bell pepper, orange bell pepper

24 medium shrimp, grilled or boiled, peeled, deveined

Fresh basil leaves for garnish

① Mix mayonnaise, pesto sauce and basil in a small bowl.

② Heat the broiler. Place bread slices on a baking sheet. Very lightly brush oil over each slice of bread. Broil the bread, 6 inches from heat, until lightly toasted, about 1 minute.

③ Spread the pesto mixture over one side of each bread slice. Top each with a small pile of julienned peppers and then a shrimp. Garnish with basil leaves and serve.

olive-avocado dim sum

makes 40 pieces
prep: 20 minutes / chill: 1 hour

THIS RECIPE FOR SEAWEED-WRAPPED AVOCADO FILLING IS PERFECT FOR APPE-
tizers. It's adapted from a recipe from Karyn Calabrese.

2 ripe avocados, peeled, seeded

½ cup each: chopped black olives, chopped onions

⅓ cup minced cilantro, optional

2 teaspoons each: ground cumin, chopped fresh ginger root, minced garlic, minced jalapeno pepper

Juice of 1 lemon

10 sheets nori seaweed wrap, see note

① Mix together all ingredients except nori; refrigerate at least 1 hour. Meanwhile, cut each nori sheet into 4 pieces. Pleat pieces into muffin tins to form cups. Fill each cup with about 1½ tablespoons of the avocado mixture.

NOTE: Nori sheets, made from dried seaweed, are most well-known as a wrap for sushi. They are available in Asian markets and Asian food sections in some supermarkets.

asian summer rolls

makes 8 pieces

prep: 25 minutes / cook: 4 minutes

KIM NGUYEN CAME TO THE STATES FROM LAOS AS A SMALL CHILD IN 1975. Now, she stays busy at Pasteur, her Chicago restaurant. Nguyen inspired us to create a light and satisfying roll wrapped in rice paper. Our recipe provides a road map, but feel free to vary your route as she suggests.

- 2 ounces thin rice noodles, see note
- 2 tablespoons each: chopped basil, cilantro, mint
- 8 sheets (8½-inch diameter each) rice paper, see note
- 8 peeled cooked shrimp, halved lengthwise
- 1 carrot, peeled, grated
- 2 tablespoons chopped dry-roasted peanuts

- ¼ cup water
- 1 tablespoon plus 1 teaspoon fish sauce, see note
- Juice of 1 lime
- 1 clove garlic, minced
- 1 tablespoon sugar
- ½ teaspoon crushed red pepper

① Heat a medium saucepan of water to a boil over medium-high heat; add rice noodles. Cook until the noodles are al dente, about 4 minutes. Drain noodles, reserving the water.

② Combine the basil, cilantro and mint in a small bowl; set aside. Pour some of the boiling water from the noodles into a large shallow dish. Dip 1 wrapper into the water for 2 seconds to soften. Transfer to a dish towel covered with plastic wrap.

③ Place 2 shrimp halves laid head to tail, a handful of rice noodles, 2 teaspoons of the herb mixture, carrot and peanuts in a row across the bottom third of the wrapper. Roll the paper up over the filling; fold in each side. Tightly roll up. Repeat with the remaining rice paper wrappers and fillings. (Wrap in plastic wrap and refrigerate if not serving immediately.)

④ Combine water, fish sauce, lime juice, garlic, sugar and crushed red pepper in a small bowl; divide dipping sauce between 4 ramekins or custard cups. Serve with wraps.

NOTE: Look for rice paper sheets, rice noodles and fish sauce in Asian stores and the Asian section of specialty stores such as Whole Foods Market.

creamy basil-onion dip

makes about 1 cup

prep: 15 minutes / cook: 35 minutes / chill: 30 minutes

Whsh did dip become a joke? Clearly it was after the great dip rush of the early '50s, which began when a recipe for clam dip presented on television's "Kraft Music Hall" caused such excitement that the next day New York City sold out of canned clams. This dip from Renee Enna was inspired in equal parts by recipes from two cookbook authors: Sally Sampson and her caramelized onion dip and Betty Rosbottom and her basil mayonnaise.

2 tablespoons olive oil

1 large sweet onion, thinly sliced

1 clove garlic, minced

1 tablespoon balsamic vinegar

⅔ cup light mayonnaise

⅓ cup low-fat yogurt, preferably Greek

¼ cup finely chopped basil

Freshly ground pepper

① Heat the oil in a large skillet over medium heat; add the onion. Cook, stirring often, until caramelized, about 30 minutes. Add the garlic and vinegar; cook, stirring, until garlic softens, about 5 minutes.

② Pour the onion-garlic mixture into a small bowl; stir in the mayonnaise, yogurt, basil and pepper to taste. Refrigerate 30 minutes.

vegetable-stuffed deviled eggs

serves 4

prep: 20 minutes / chill: 2 hours

THESE COOL DEVILED EGGS MAKE A REFRESHING SUMMER SNACK. A TWIST ON A classic, these cool deviled eggs make for a refreshing summer snack, with the crunch of fresh garden vegetables.

- 4 hard-cooked eggs, chilled, peeled, halved lengthwise
- 1 teaspoon prepared mustard
- 2 tablespoons mayonnaise
- ½ clove garlic, minced

- 1 cup finely diced garden vegetables (carrots, green onions, onions, celery, cucumber, zucchini, radishes, etc.)
- Salt, pepper to taste

① Mix the yolks from eggs with mustard, mayonnaise, garlic, chopped vegetables, salt and pepper to taste. Mound into the hollow of each half of egg white. Chill.

cheese and rye cocktail sandwiches

makes 22 sandwiches
prep: 30 minutes / cook: 1 minute

A SURE BET WITH GUESTS ARE BITE-SIZE SANDWICHES, WHICH CAN BE HELD between two fingers and nibbled at elegantly or dispatched in one swoop. Here, then, is a tiny sandwich—complete with lettuce!—that delighted all the Good Eating staff when we tasted it. The recipe is guaranteed to work magic at your party as well.

¼ cup mayonnaise

1 teaspoon Dijon mustard

¼ teaspoon paprika

1 loaf (1 pound) party cocktail rye bread

1 pound Gruyere cheese, grated

Lettuce

2 baby whole dill pickles, minced

① Heat broiler. Combine mayonnaise, mustard and paprika in a small mixing bowl. Spread mayonnaise mixture on one side of each bread slice. Place bread slices on a baking sheet. Sprinkle with grated cheese.

② Broil until cheese melts, about 1 minute. Remove from oven. Top half of the bread slices with lettuce and pickles. Top with remaining slices; press down. Cut in half; serve warm.

mexican pinwheels

makes about 4 dozen bite-size pieces
prep: 15 minutes / chill: several hours

ANY EVENT CAN BECOME A FIESTA WITH THE RIGHT MIX OF FLAVORS. START your fiesta with this spicy appetizer from Lois Starkey of Norridge.

¾ cup thick salsa	2–3 tablespoons chopped onion
1 package (8 ounces) cream cheese or light cream cheese	5–6 drops hot pepper sauce
2 cups (8 ounces) shredded Cheddar cheese	6 flour tortillas

① Put the salsa in a strainer and set aside to drain for 10 minutes. Transfer drained salsa to a food processor or blender. Add cream cheese, Cheddar cheese, onion and hot pepper sauce. Mix until smooth.

② Spread mixture over tortillas and roll into cylinders. Wrap in plastic wrap; refrigerate at least 2 hours. Cut into thin slices.

chilled white gazpacho

serves 6

prep: 30 minutes / chill: 6–8 hours

pictured on p. 42

"YOU'RE LESS HUNGRY WHEN IT IS SUPER HOT," SAYS LEE WOLEN, EXECUTIVE chef/partner at Boka restaurant. The grapes and strawberries in this chilled soup sweeten it, while the sherry vinegar counters with acidity, he says. Toasted almonds, both pureed and sliced, add texture. The pureed nuts provide creaminess.

- 4 cups green grapes
- 2½ cups English cucumber, peeled and diced, 1 cup reserved
- 1 cup almonds, toasted (see note), ½ cup reserved
- ¼ cup green pepper, seeded and diced
- ¼ cup baguette, crust removed and cubed
- 2 sprigs tarragon
- ¼ cup olive oil
- 4 tablespoons sherry vinegar
- 1 teaspoon salt
- ½ cup sliced strawberries

① Combine all ingredients, except the reserved cucumber, strawberries and reserved almonds, in a large bowl and allow to marinate for 6 to 8 hours in the refrigerator until the bread is completely soft and soggy from the oil and vinegar. Remove the tarragon sprigs.

② Puree the soup in a blender on high speed until smooth. (Thin with a little water, if needed.) Strain. Chill. Adjust seasoning to taste.

③ Garnish the soup right before serving with the reserved cucumber, the strawberries and the reserved almonds. Serve with a crusty baguette.

NOTE: To toast almonds, place in a dry skillet set over medium heat until golden, about 3 to 5 minutes. Stir occasionally to avoid scorching.

pecorino crisp

serves 15 to 20

prep: 1 hour / dehydrate: 4 hours / cook: 40 minutes

CHICAGO'S 42 GRAMS CHEF JAKE BICKELHAUPT'S INTENSELY SCULPTURAL white-on-white-on-white pecorino cheese crisp is both show-stopping in presentation and, in the chef's words, an "extreme burst of flavor." A challenge for the cook, but one that pays dividends in flavor and the inevitable awe once your guests get a look at what's coming out of your kitchen. The artful offering is meant to be picked up and nibbled. Bickelhaupt says you can fry the crisps a couple of days ahead of time and keep in an airtight container until the party. If they soften a bit, put them in a 325-degree oven for four to five minutes.

PECORINO STOCK:
8 ounces pecorino cheese
1 gallon water

PECORINO CRISP:
1 pint (2 cups) ground tapioca pearls
Oil for deep frying

PECORINO FONDUE:
¼ cup shredded pecorino
1 quart heavy cream

PECORINO FOAM:
½ cup skim milk

① Make the stock. Cut the cheese into small cubes and place in a large stockpot with the water. Bring to a boil and then turn off heat. Steep 30 minutes. Strain through a fine mesh sieve. Refrigerate until needed.

② Make the crisps. Finely grind tapioca. Blend 2 quarts of stock and ground tapioca pearls in a blender in batches, or whisk by hand. Pour mixture into a large stockpot on medium-high heat. Cook, stirring often with a whisk, until the mixture becomes thick and viscous, about 20 minutes.

③ Spread mixture to about ⅛-inch thick on dehydrator trays lined with a nonstick baking sheets. Place all trays in the dehydrator and dry at 145 degrees for 3 hours. When the sheets aren't tacky to the touch, carefully pull them from the baking sheets and flip over to the other side. Dry for an additional 1–2 hours until completely dry but still pliable. Or oven-dry using silicone baking mats on baking sheets. Set the oven temperature as low as possible and monitor closely as drying time may differ.

④ Heat oil in a large saucepan to 365 degrees. Break the pecorino sheets into pieces approximately the size of a playing card. Fry the pecorino sheets in batches until they puff up; it takes only a few seconds. Keep the crisps as white as possible. Blot on paper towel. Repeat until all sheets are fried. Set aside.

⑤ Make fondue. Place shredded cheese and heavy cream in a saucepan. Cook on medium heat until simmering. Stir frequently. Pour fondue into a pastry bag or plastic squeeze bottle. Leave out at room temperature until needed.

⑥ Make the pecorino foam right before serving. Place 1 quart of stock and the milk in a large pot. Using an immersion blender or hand whisk, beat to create a foam.

⑦ Assemble dish. Squeeze 3 pea-size dots of fondue onto a crisp. Repeat for all crisps. Add a tablespoon or two of foam to each crisp.

prosciutto wrapped figs

makes 16 pieces
prep: 10 minutes

THERE ARE TWO SEASONS FOR FRESH FIGS, A SHORT ONE IN EARLY SUMMER AND a second one beginning in late summer and extending through fall. This simple dish by Chef Jared Case, formerly of Prasino, elevates the fig to its finest with only a few ingredients that enhance its beauty.

4–8 **fresh figs, halved and stem removed (quartered if large)**
Aged balsamic

Manchego cheese, shaved
16 **thinly cut prosciutto slices**

① Drizzle a few drops of balsamic on the flesh of the figs. Place a shaving of manchego on the figs and wrap each in a prosciutto slice.

refreshing eats

SIDE AND ENTREE SALADS

empress coleslaw p. 70
italian slaw for a crowd p. 72
baked potato salad p. 73
red, white and blue potato salad p. 75
fingerling potato salad with tarragon p. 76
potato salad nicoise p. 79
curried sweet potato salad with golden raisins and toasted almonds p. 80
lentil salad with lemon dressing p. 81
wild rice salad with fennel and mustard dressing p. 82
pasta salad with shallots, herbs and tomato compote p. 84
roasted pepper and onion salad with goat cheese and orange p. 85
marshall field's lemon pasta salad p. 87
roasted vegetable salad with apple vinaigrette p. 89
summer salad with fresh citrus vinaigrette p. 90
abundant sorrel salad p. 92
asparagus salad with red onion, tomato and basil p. 94
cauliflower and red pepper salad with sweet mustard dressing p. 95
asian salad of sugar snap peas, mushrooms and cilantro leaves p. 96
swiss cheese salad p. 97
mixed greens with marinated flank steak and herb vinaigrette p. 98
« quick crab and avocado salad p. 99
hot or cold beef-soba noodle salad p. 100
summer bean salad with sun gold tomatoes, herbs, smoked trout, goat cheese dressing p. 102
grilled shrimp and pineapple salad p. 105
napa slaw with charred salmon p. 106
seared scallops with a fennel, olive and red onion salad p. 107
papa eloy's tuna salad p. 108
new nicoise salad p. 111
spinach and fingerling potato salad with warm bacon dressing p. 112
chioggia beet salad p. 115
beet carpaccio p. 117

empress coleslaw

serves 4

prep: 20 minutes

To CREATE SLAW AT HOME, THE COOK NEEDS ONLY A LARGE CHEF'S KNIFE OR A box grater. Another option is the food processor's shredding or slicing blade and the countless chopping devices advertised on late-night television. If you like, serve this Asian-style slaw topped with chopped cooked chicken or shrimp. It was developed in the Tribune test kitchen by William Rice.

½ head Chinese cabbage, thinly sliced

2 ribs celery, thinly sliced

2 green onions, minced

½ teaspoon fennel or anise seed, crushed

1 piece (2 inches) ginger root, minced, optional

1 teaspoon salt

½ teaspoon ground white pepper

¼ cup mayonnaise

2 tablespoons peanut oil

1 tablespoon sherry vinegar

① Mix cabbage and celery in a medium bowl. Combine green onions, fennel seed, ginger, salt and pepper in a small bowl. Add mayonnaise; stir to combine ingredients. Slowly stir in oil and vinegar.

② Pour dressing over cabbage and celery; toss to blend. Chill if desired.

italian slaw for a crowd

serves 20

prep: 35 minutes / cook: 6 minutes / stand: 1 hour

C HEF DAVID SHEA HAS NOSTALGIC MEMORIES OF HIS FAMILY'S SLAW: "AS A KID, I spent summers on a farm in the Hudson River Valley and coleslaw was a standby. It was pretty traditional: green cabbage, celery and carrot with a creamy dressing made with commercial mayonnaise, of course, and a little mustard. At about age 10, I was allowed to chop the cabbage. My knife skills were lacking, but the slaw tasted OK... I eliminate the mayo, use two types of vinegar to brighten the flavor and add onion and heirloom tomatoes for color and texture."

1 head each, outer leaves removed, cored: green cabbage, red cabbage

¼ cup each: red wine vinegar, balsamic vinegar

3 tablespoons mustard, grainy preferred

¾ cup extra-virgin olive oil

4 large tomatoes, chopped

1 large bunch basil, leaves torn into pieces

1 large red onion, cut into ¼-inch slices

¼ teaspoon salt or to taste

Freshly ground pepper

① Quarter the cabbages; slice as thinly as possible. Transfer to a large bowl. Whisk vinegars and mustard in a small bowl; slowly whisk in ½ cup of the olive oil. Season with salt and pepper; set aside.

② Heat an oiled grill pan or skillet. Sear the onions until just browned, about 6 minutes; add to cabbage. Pour dressing over cabbage; set aside for 1 hour.

③ Mix together tomatoes, basil and remaining ¼ cup of the olive oil in medium bowl; add to the cabbage mixture. Toss gently to mix.

baked potato salad

serves 6

prep: 20 minutes / cook: 30 minutes / chill: 1 hour

THIS RECIPE USES FAVORITE BAKED POTATO TOPPINGS AND TURNS THEM INTO a dressing for a potato salad. How to boil a potato? Don't laugh; not everyone knows the proper way to do it. Make sure all the potatoes are the same size; if large and small potatoes are mixed together, they will cook unevenly. Or, if you must use mixed sizes, add the smaller potatoes to the pot later so they don't overcook. Scrub the outside of the potato to remove grit and any small growths. Use the tip of a paring knife to cut out green spots or the "eyes." If potatoes are left unpeeled, it will be easy to remove the skin after boiling. If the potatoes are peeled first, place peeled potatoes in a bowl of cold water to prevent discoloration while peeling the rest. Potatoes should not be left in water more than two hours, however, or they may lose water-soluble nutrients. Put the potatoes in a large saucepan covered by at least 1 inch of cold salted water. Heat to a vigorous boil, reduce heat and boil uncovered at least 15 minutes, depending on the size of the potato. Test for doneness by inserting a thin knife into the potato. It should slide in easily.

2 pounds new white potatoes

2 tablespoons red wine vinegar

¼ cup sour cream

2 tablespoons each: plain yogurt, milk

Salt, freshly ground pepper

6 strips thick-cut bacon, cooked, crumbled

½ cup chopped chives

① Cover potatoes with cold water; heat to boil. Cook, uncovered, until potatoes are tender when pierced with a knife, about 20 minutes. Drain; set aside to cool slightly.

② Quarter potatoes while still warm. Place in medium serving bowl. Toss potatoes with vinegar; set aside.

③ Blend sour cream, yogurt, milk and salt and pepper to taste in small bowl. Add to potatoes; toss to coat. Mix in bacon and chives. Refrigerate salad for at least 1 hour. Bring to room temperature before serving.

red, white and blue potato salad

serves 6

prep: 15 minutes / cook: 30 minutes / chill: 1 hour

IF YOU'RE FEELING ESPECIALLY PATRIOTIC, FIND PURPLE POTATOES AT A FARMERS market or a store with a well-stocked produce department to add the "blue" to this salad, developed in the Tribune test kitchen. The color is the most interesting thing about these potatoes; the flavor can range from slightly sweet to nutty. Not all purple potatoes are colored through and through; some have purple skin and white interiors. The potatoes vary in starch content, which affects their texture; be sure to avoid overcooking if the potatoes are to be used in salads.

¾ pound each: red, purple, new white potatoes

2 tablespoons red wine vinegar

½ cup mayonnaise

2 tablespoons Dijon mustard

2 each, chopped: green onions, celery ribs

¼ cup minced parsley

½ teaspoon each: salt, freshly ground pepper

① Place potatoes in large pot; fill with cold water to cover. Heat to boil; simmer, until potatoes are tender when pierced with a knife, about 20 minutes. Drain; set aside to cool slightly.

② Cut potatoes into quarters while still warm. Place in medium serving bowl. Toss potatoes with vinegar. Mix together mayonnaise, mustard, green onions, celery, parsley, salt and pepper in a small bowl. Toss with potatoes. Refrigerate at least 1 hour. Bring to room temperature before serving.

fingerling potato salad with tarragon

serves 6

prep: 15 minutes / cook: 30 minutes

THE TENDER LITTLE POTATOES KNOWN AS FINGERLINGS HAVE A CREAMY texture that needs little embellishment. Short and knubby, like some fingers, these potatoes have become increasingly available in recent years, especially at farmers markets and natural food stores. The slightly waxy flesh of the potatoes, with names such as French and Russian banana, may be white or yellow, covered by a thin skin that can be eaten. This recipe, developed in the Tribune test kitchen, gives the potatoes a mild dressing that is fragrant with fresh tarragon.

2 pounds fingerling potatoes

3 tablespoons tarragon vinegar or white wine vinegar

1 tablespoon Dijon mustard

½ teaspoon each: salt, freshly ground pepper

½ cup extra-virgin olive oil

1 each, minced: shallot, clove garlic

2 tablespoons minced parsley

1 tablespoon minced tarragon

① Place potatoes in large pot; fill with cold water to cover. Heat to boil; simmer until potatoes are tender when pierced with thin end of knife, about 15 minutes. Drain; set aside to cool slightly. Slice.

② Toss potatoes with 2 tablespoons of the vinegar. Whisk together remaining vinegar, mustard, salt and pepper in small bowl. Slowly whisk in olive oil. Add shallot and garlic; whisk to combine. Pour over potatoes; gently toss to coat. Add parsley and tarragon; toss. Serve at room temperature.

potato salad nicoise

serves 6

prep: 30 minutes / cook: 25 minutes

ONE OF THE GREAT THINGS ABOUT BEING AN AMERICAN IS BEING ABLE TO reinvent yourself—even if you're everyone's favorite picnic side dish, potato salad. A classic salade Nicoise, named for the city of Nice in the south of France, is a composed plate with the ingredients in this recipe. Here, they have been mixed together to make a lively potato salad.

- 2 pounds new red potatoes
- 4 ounces thin green beans, cut into ½-inch pieces
- 1 can (6 ounces) albacore tuna, drained
- 1 large tomato, peeled, seeded, diced
- 1 anchovy fillet, minced

- ½ cup pitted, sliced black Kalamata olives
- 1 tablespoon each: white wine vinegar, minced parsley
- 2 teaspoons Dijon mustard
- ¼ cup extra-virgin olive oil
- ½ shallot, minced
  Salt, freshly ground pepper
- 2 hard-cooked eggs, sliced

① Place potatoes and salt in large pot; fill with cold water to cover. Heat to boil; simmer potatoes until tender, about 18 minutes. Add green beans; cook 2 minutes. Drain; set aside to cool slightly. Cut potatoes into quarters. Place potatoes, beans, tuna, tomato, anchovy and olives in large bowl; toss to combine. Set aside.

② Whisk together vinegar, parsley and mustard in small bowl; slowly whisk in oil. Whisk in shallot and salt and pepper to taste. Pour over potato mixture; gently toss to coat. Garnish with eggs.

curried sweet potato salad with golden raisins and toasted almonds

serves 6

prep: 25 minutes / cook: 10 minutes

SWEET POTATOES ADD A NICE FLAVOR AND PRETTY COLOR TO SALADS BUT become mushy if overcooked. Boil them only until soft. This potato salad has an Indian twist, with a sweet and spicy curried dressing.

2 pounds sweet potatoes, peeled, diced

½ cup each: yogurt, mayonnaise

1 tablespoon curry powder

1 piece (1 inch) fresh ginger root, minced

1 teaspoon brown sugar

½ cup golden raisins

⅓ cup sliced almonds, toasted, see note

4 green onions, chopped

Salt, freshly ground pepper

① Place potatoes in large pot; fill with cold water to cover. Heat to boil; simmer potatoes until tender, about 7 minutes. Drain, set aside.

② Combine yogurt, mayonnaise, curry powder, ginger root and brown sugar in medium bowl. Add potatoes, raisins, almonds, onions and salt and pepper to taste; toss to coat.

NOTE: To toast almonds, place in small, dry skillet over medium heat, stirring frequently, until golden, about 6 minutes.

pasta salad with shallots, herbs and tomato compote

serves 4

prep: 10 minutes / stand: 10 minutes / cook: 6 minutes

SHALLOTS AND TOMATO COMPOTE MAKE THIS PASTA SALAD MAGNIFIQUE! Prepare this salad well in advance and allow it to rest, which lets the flavors merge.

1 package (9 ounces) fresh fettuccine, cooked

3 tablespoons extra-virgin olive oil

1 tablespoon white wine vinegar

2 medium shallots, minced

1 tablespoon each: drained capers, whipping cream

1 teaspoon fresh lemon juice
Salt, ground red pepper to taste

3 tablespoons finely minced mixed fresh herbs

1 cup small cherry tomatoes, quartered lengthwise

1 small clove garlic, minced

① Place hot, drained pasta in a mixing bowl and immediately toss with 2½ tablespoons of the oil, the vinegar and shallots. Let stand until pasta is cool, about 10 minutes.

② Add capers, cream, lemon juice, salt, red pepper and herbs; mix well.

③ In another bowl, lightly toss tomatoes with garlic, remaining ½ tablespoon oil, salt and red pepper.

④ To serve, mound the pasta on a small platter and place the tomato mixture in the center. Serve at room temperature.

roasted pepper and onion salad with goat cheese and orange

serves 6

prep: 15 minutes / cook: 15 minutes

THE SWEETNESS OF ROASTED PEPPERS AND ORANGES IS A BEAUTIFUL CONTRAST against the sharp goat cheese in this salad.

1 tablespoon plus 2 teaspoons olive oil

1 large Vidalia or other sweet onion, cut in ¼-inch wedges

3 tablespoons orange juice

Salt, ground red pepper to taste

2 teaspoons minced fresh tarragon

4 bell peppers, either all red or a mix of red, yellow and green, roasted

1 tablespoon red wine vinegar

4 large leaves red leaf lettuce

½ cup diced, peeled orange

¼ cup crumbled French goat cheese

① Heat 2 teaspoons of the oil in a nonstick skillet over high heat. Add onion wedges and cook, stirring often, until soft, 5 minutes. Add 1 tablespoon of the orange juice, salt and a large dash of red pepper. Cook 1 minute longer, remove from heat and add half the tarragon. Set aside to cool.

② Cut roasted peppers into strips. Combine with remaining 1 tablespoon oil, 2 tablespoons orange juice and tarragon. Add vinegar, salt and red pepper. Mix well.

③ To serve, arrange lettuce on a serving plate and top with onions then peppers. Scatter orange pieces over and add cheese.

marshall field's lemon pasta salad

serves 8

prep: 20 minutes / cook: 11 minutes / chill: 2 hours

MACY'S HERE IN CHICAGO HAD A PREVIOUS LIFE, AS MARSHALL FIELD'S. THIS was one of the many well-loved dishes that devoted Field's shoppers often picked up by the pound in the venerable store's food court. Kathy Finn of Evanston was one of those loyal shoppers. "Back in the early '90s when my office was located just a few blocks from State Street, I got hooked on a zesty lemony pasta salad filled with fresh basil, tomatoes and grated Parmesan cheese ... at the former Marshall Field's lower-level food court," Finn wrote. "When my office moved to the suburbs, I wrote to Marshall Field's and explained my plight. They responded with a letter of thanks, the recipe for my favorite salad and a 1-pound box of Frango Mints ... My friends and I have been making it ever since." Based on tasters' comments, we made the dried basil optional.

1 pound rotini

Grated zest of 2 lemons

½ cup olive oil

⅓ cup fresh lemon juice

1 teaspoon each, or to taste: salt, freshly ground pepper

3 tomatoes, cored, chopped

1 bunch fresh basil leaves, chopped

1 cup shredded Parmesan cheese

¼ cup dried basil, optional

① Cook pasta according to package directions.

② Meanwhile, combine the lemon zest, olive oil, lemon juice, salt and pepper in a bowl; set aside. Drain pasta; transfer to large bowl. Pour lemon-oil mixture over warm pasta. Toss; cover. Refrigerate 1 hour.

③ Stir in the tomatoes, fresh basil, cheese and dried basil. Cover; refrigerate 1 hour. Toss lightly before serving.

abundant sorrel salad

serves 4
prep: 15 minutes

SORREL PROVOKES PUCKER. IT'S LEMON-SOUR, TANGY-TART, WHICH IS WHY the bold green with the bold plan for garden domination so often gets ground down to fish sauce. On this salad, it's the star.

1 ripe, juicy tomato	Basil
Olive oil	Parsley
Flaky salt, such as Maldon	Thyme
Freshly ground black pepper	Dill, optional
Sorrel	Chives
Lettuce	

① Grate tomato on the large holes of a box-grater, discarding skin. Scrape tomato and juices into a salad bowl. Stir in 3 tablespoons olive oil, ½ teaspoon salt and ¼ teaspoon pepper.

② Break stems off sorrel and discard. Wash and spin-dry leaves. Slice crosswise into thin strips. Measure 2 cups and drop into the salad bowl.

③ Wash and dry lettuce. If leaves are small, use them whole. If not, cut down to about 2-inch bites. Measure 2 cups and drop into salad bowl.

④ Wash and dry whole basil leaves, parsley leaves, thyme leaves, dill (snipped to 1-inch tufts) and chives (snipped to ½-inch spears). Measure 2 cups of these mixed herbs and drop into salad bowl. Toss well.

⑤ Taste. Drizzle with more oil and scatter on more salt if need be. Heap onto plates. Enjoy.

asparagus salad with red onion, tomato and basil

serves 2–4

prep: 20 minutes / cook: 10 minutes

THIS SALAD IS DELICIOUS AND MAKES THE MOST OF THE ASPARAGUS AND BASIL that's so abundant in late summer.

- 1 pound asparagus, bottoms trimmed, peeled, see note
- 2 tablespoons olive oil
- ⅛ teaspoon salt
  Freshly ground black pepper
- 2 teaspoons balsamic vinegar

- 1 teaspoon red wine vinegar
- ¾ teaspoon sugar
- ¼ cup diced tomato
- 2 tablespoons slivered fresh basil leaves
- 1 tablespoon diced red onion

① Heat large skillet filled with salted water to boil. Add asparagus; simmer, uncovered, until just tender, about 10 minutes. Drain; blot asparagus with paper towels. Place asparagus in bowl; toss with olive oil, salt and pepper.

② When ready to serve, add vinegars, sugar, tomato, basil and onion. Toss. Taste; adjust seasoning. Arrange attractively on small platter. Serve hot, at room temperature or chilled.

NOTE: To peel spears, lay each spear on board. Use sharp swivel-bladed vegetable peeler to peel stems, rotating spear on board until stem is peeled.

cauliflower and red pepper salad with sweet mustard dressing

serves 6

prep: 20 minutes / cook: 30 seconds

THE SWEETNESS OF THE DRESSING IN THIS SALAD IS A LOVELY COUNTERPOINT to the fresh, hearty vegetables.

1 head cauliflower, florets only

1 red bell pepper, diced

⅓ cup canola oil

2 tablespoons each: Dijon mustard, honey

1 tablespoon each: lemon juice, white wine vinegar

⅛ teaspoon salt

Freshly ground black pepper

① Heat large pot of salted water to boil. Add cauliflower, cook 30 seconds. Drain; blot with paper towels. Place in medium bowl. Add red pepper, oil, mustard, honey, lemon juice, vinegar, salt and pepper. Toss well. Taste; adjust seasoning. Serve chilled or at room temperature.

asian salad of sugar snap peas, mushrooms and cilantro leaves

serves 4

prep: 20 minutes / cook: 30 seconds

YOU'LL LOVE THE COMBINATION OF GINGER AND SUGAR SNAP PEAS WITH THIS salad's sesame oil and a taste of honey.

1 pound small sugar snap peas

7 green onions, thinly sliced

2 teaspoons minced fresh ginger root

1 teaspoon sesame oil

½ teaspoon salt

½ pound small cremini or button mushrooms, stems trimmed, sliced

¼ cup cilantro leaves

2 tablespoons each: seasoned rice wine vinegar, fresh lemon juice, peanut oil

1 tablespoon honey

① Heat large pot of salted water to boil. Add sugar snap peas. Cook 30 seconds; drain. Place in large bowl; stir in green onions. Toss with ginger, sesame oil and salt. Can be prepared a day ahead and refrigerated.

② To serve, add mushrooms, cilantro, vinegar, lemon juice, peanut oil and honey. Toss until well mixed. Taste; adjust seasoning with vinegar and lemon juice. Let rest 10 minutes.

quick crab and avocado salad

serves 6
prep: 20 minutes
pictured on p. 68

Once an odd-sounding combination, crab married with avocado and grapefruit is now everywhere from the Food Network to neighborhood luncheons. But the flavor created here might surprise those expecting a typical crab salad. Instead of mayo, we substituted avocado, which provides the same creamy texture. A touch of horseradish enhances the citrus flavor, and a sprinkling of sliced almonds delivers crunch. Like a twice-baked potato, the salad is served in a shell. But unlike a twice-baked potato, the avocado spends little time outside of its skin. It is simply mixed with crab, grapefruit and horseradish before it returns home. The taste and the look is intricate, but the process is simple.

3 ripe avocados, halved, pitted, in their shell

Juice of 1 lemon

2 tablespoons horseradish sauce

1 grapefruit, peeled, sectioned, sections cut in half

8 ounces jumbo lump crab meat, picked through to remove shell pieces

½ cup sliced, roasted almonds

① Carefully scoop out avocados into a medium bowl, leaving some of the fruit still lining the shell. Set shells aside.

② Add half of the lemon juice and horseradish sauce to the avocados; mix until smooth. Stir in the sectioned grapefruit; fold in the crab.

③ Brush the avocado shells with the remaining lemon juice. Fill shells with the mixture; top with almonds. Keep chilled until ready to serve.

hot or cold beef-soba noodle salad

serves 4
prep: 25 minutes / cook: 11 minutes

THIS RECIPE USES JAPANESE SOBA NOODLES, MADE OF BUCKWHEAT AND WHEAT, which add heft to an entree salad. These are sold in many supermarkets, as well as ethnic and specialty stores. (However, spaghetti noodles will work just fine.) Hoisin is a sweet-salty sauce made of soybeans, garlic, chilies and other spices. It's sold in ethnic stores and some larger supermarkets. If you can't find it, you can substitute an additional 2 tablespoons soy sauce for the recipe here.

When buying ginger, look for blemish-free flesh. To mince, cut a large chunk off the knob; peel off the papery, outer layer; cut that chunk into thin slices, and then mince.

1 package (8 ounces) soba noodles or spaghetti

2 tablespoons peanut or vegetable oil

1 teaspoon sesame oil, optional

4 green onions, chopped

2 cloves garlic, minced

1 piece (1-inch) fresh ginger root, peeled, minced

1 beef strip steak (about 8 ounces), cut into strips

2 tablespoons each: low-sodium soy sauce, hoisin sauce

2 tomatoes, cut into large chunks, or 16 cherry tomatoes, halved

¼ pound snow peas or string beans

2 tablespoons minced fresh basil or mint

1 bag (10 ounces) mesclun or herb-blend salad greens

¼ cup coarsely chopped peanuts

① Heat water to a boil in stockpot; cook noodles according to package directions. Meanwhile, heat peanut and sesame oil in skillet over medium heat. Add green onions, garlic and ginger; cook until fragrant and slightly soft, about 2 minutes. Add beef; cook, stirring occasionally, until meat is cooked to desired doneness, about 4 minutes for medium. Add soy and hoisin sauces, tomatoes and snow peas; cook, stirring constantly, until vegetables soften, about 5 minutes. Stir in basil; remove from heat.

② Drain noodles; combine with beef mixture. (If you prefer a cold salad, store noodle-beef mixture in covered container in refrigerator until ready to use.) Divide salad greens among four plates or bowls; put noodle-beef mixture on top. Top each serving with 1 teaspoon chopped peanuts.

summer bean salad with sun gold tomatoes, herbs, smoked trout, goat cheese dressing

serves 4
prep: 40 minutes / cook: 1 minute

CHEF JASON HAMMEL, CO-OWNER/CHEF OF LULA CAFE AND CO-OWNER OF Nightwood Restaurant, contributed this recipe to "The Green City Market Cookbook" (Agate Midway, $24.99). The book, created by the sustainable market of that name in Lincoln Park, is full of recipes (arranged by season) inspired by market produce. The inspiration for Hammel's dish hit him in a way that is the best approach to shopping any farmers market—he let what looked the best dictate the menu.

2 ¼ teaspoons salt

½ pound mixed pole beans, such as yellow, green, haricots verts, etc.

2 small pattypan squash, sliced on a mandoline or very thinly sliced

2 radishes, sliced on a mandoline or very thinly sliced

½ cup Sun Gold cherry tomatoes, quartered or halved

2 tablespoons extra-virgin olive oil

2 teaspoons red wine vinegar or Champagne vinegar

¼ cup chopped mixed fresh herbs, such as tarragon, thyme, basil and chives

¼ cup sour cream

¼ cup buttermilk

1 small shallot, minced

1 tablespoon honey

1½ teaspoons cider vinegar

1 teaspoon Dijon mustard

½ cup crumbled goat cheese

3 ounces smoked trout, broken into chunks

① Place a bowl of ice water next to the sink.

② Fill a large stockpot with water; place it over high heat. Add 2 teaspoons salt; heat to a rolling boil. Add the beans; simmer, 30 seconds to 1 minute. Remove stockpot from the heat.

③ Drain the beans; plunge them into the ice water bath to cool. Drain, pat dry with a paper towel; cut the beans on the bias into ½-inch slices.

④ Toss together the beans, squash, radishes, tomatoes, oil, red wine vinegar and the remaining ¼ teaspoon salt in a large bowl. Add the herbs; toss again.

⑤ In a separate bowl, combine the sour cream, buttermilk, shallot, honey, cider vinegar and mustard; mix well. Stir in the goat cheese.

⑥ Spoon the dressing onto four serving plates. Top with the bean mixture and smoked trout and serve.

grilled shrimp and pineapple salad

serves 4

prep: 15 minutes / cook: 5 minutes

HERE'S A MAIN-DISH SALAD THAT TAKES A LIGHT APPROACH AND A TROPICAL bent, starting with grilled tail-on shrimp and pineapple. Dressing the skewers, and the salad, is a combination of ingredients that will inspire summer thoughts, whatever the temperature happens to be outside. We're adding another layer of flavor by topping the salad greens with a generous dose of chopped, fresh mint. We recommend skewering the shrimp and pineapple separately; cooking time may vary slightly between the two ingredients, and this will give you more control. Besides, the food will be removed from the skewers before serving. Five-spice powder, also called Chinese five-spice powder, is available in the spice aisle of many supermarkets. But you could substitute ¼ teaspoon allspice.

20 tail-on raw shrimp, thawed if frozen

1 can (20 ounces) pineapple chunks in juice

½ cup extra-virgin olive oil

2 tablespoons pineapple juice (from liquid in can)

1 tablespoon honey

1 tablespoon rice wine vinegar

¼ teaspoon each: salt, five-spice powder

1 bag (8 ounces) mixed baby greens

½ cup each or to taste: chopped fresh mint, chow mein noodles

① Skewer the shrimp and pineapple chunks on separate metal skewers; set aside. Combine the oil, pineapple juice, honey, rice wine vinegar, salt and five-spice powder in a measuring cup.

② Heat a grill to medium-high heat. Pour about 3 tablespoons of the oil-vinegar mixture into a ramekin; brush the shrimp and pineapple with the mixture. (Note: Discard any excess mixture from ramekin because it has been in contact with the raw fish.) Grill until shrimp is opaque and pineapple has caramelized, 3–5 minutes.

③ Divide the greens into four shallow bowls; sprinkle 2 tablespoons mint over each. Divide the shrimp and pineapple among each bowl; top with chow mein noodles. Dress with remaining dressing.

napa slaw with charred salmon

serves 4

prep: 1 hour / cook: 10 minutes

THIS SIMPLE VINEGAR-AND-SUGAR COLESLAW MADE WITH LEAFY NAPA CABBAGE is topped with flaked salmon fillet to create a main-course salad. It was devised by the late chef and restaurateur Michael Altenberg.

3 shallots, coarsely chopped

3 tablespoons Champagne or white wine vinegar

2 tablespoons dark brown or turbinado sugar

½ teaspoon sea salt

Cracked pepper, three-color peppercorns preferred

1 each, cut into matchsticks: red, yellow bell pepper

1 carrot, peeled, cut into matchsticks

1 head napa cabbage, thinly sliced

1 bulb onion or 4 green onions (white only), chopped

1 fillet (8 ounces) salmon

1 to 2 tablespoons Dijon mustard

2 tablespoons olive oil

① Combine shallots, vinegar and sugar in a blender; puree until smooth. Add salt and pepper to taste. Combine with vegetable matchsticks and cabbage in a large bowl; toss. Season with salt and pepper. Set aside.

② Prepare a grill or heat a grill pan or broiler. Season salmon with salt and pepper. Grill 4 minutes; turn. Grill 3 minutes; brush thin film of mustard on fillet with a pastry brush. Turn; cook about 45 seconds. Brush other side with mustard; turn. Cook until medium-rare and lightly charred, about 1 minute.

③ Spread slaw on a serving platter. Flake salmon; scatter over the slaw. Drizzle olive oil over salad.

seared scallops with a fennel, olive and red onion salad

serves 6

prep: 40 minutes / stand: 20 minutes / cook: 8 minutes

THESE SEARED SCALLOPS SIT ATOP A DELICIOUS MELANGE OF SUMMER FLAVORS. This recipe is from Chef Lee Wolen of Boka restaurant.

SALAD:

1 cup Sicilian green olives (Castelvetrano olives are best)

½ cup olive oil

¼ cup fresh lemon juice

1 head fennel, sliced thin

¼ red onion, sliced thin and rinsed in ice water to reduce the raw bite

2 tablespoons each: chopped tarragon and parsley

Salt to taste

SCALLOPS:

12 sea scallops

Salt, to taste

2 tablespoons canola oil

① Place the olives between sheets of parchment paper and, using the palm of your hand, crush each olive. Discard the pits.

② In a bowl, combine the crushed olives, olive oil, lemon juice, fennel, red onion, tarragon, parsley and salt. Marinate the olives in the mixture for 20 minutes at room temperature.

③ Season the scallops with the salt. Heat a heavy-bottomed saute pan on high heat and add the canola oil to the pan.

④ Sear the scallops in the skillet until golden brown. Flip and sear on the other side until it is golden brown. Remove from heat.

⑤ Divide the salad among six plates and top each with two scallops. Serve.

papa eloy's tuna salad

serves 4
prep: 30 minutes

JOURNALIST MICHELL ELOY SHARED THE FOLLOWING STORY ABOUT HER DAD'S tuna salad: "Raised in Guadalajara, Mexico, by a Spanish Civil War refugee and an Irish-American expat, my father, Victor, consumes all forms of south-of-the-border cuisine in a seemingly vain attempt to show his European ancestors what they'd been missing out on for centuries. His solution to fixing any bland dish—be it the Thanksgiving turkey, a glass of diet cola or pasta alfredo—has always been to throw some combination of traditional Mexican ingredients in the mix. 'You know what would really make this ham and cheese sandwich better?' he'd ask my sister and me. 'A little salsa.' 'Lacking that intangible something? Nothing some avocado and lime can't fix.'

"So when my dad, after moving to Chicago for a medical internship at St. Francis Hospital in Evanston, encountered bland American tuna salad, he opted to put his own south-of-the-border spin on the oft-derided dish. What resulted is a tangy, citrusy take on an American classic that's perfect for hot summer days. Served with chips or on tostadas, the cold salad makes a great appetizer or party snack that, thanks to all the vegetables, tastes fresh and light while still packing a bit of heat."

20 ounces quality tuna in water, drained, about 4 cans

½ cup mayonnaise

3 vine-ripe tomatoes, chopped

5 to 6 green onions, chopped

¼ cup cilantro, chopped

2 avocados, peeled, cut into large pieces

1 or 2 jalapeno peppers, seeded, chopped

Juice of 2 limes

½ teaspoon salt

Freshly ground pepper

① Mix the tuna and mayonnaise in a large bowl, breaking up the tuna into smaller pieces, until evenly blended.

② Sprinkle the chopped tomatoes with a bit of salt and pepper; toss into the bowl. Add green onions, cilantro, avocados and jalapenos to the bowl. Add lime juice, salt and pepper to taste.

③ Serve as an appetizer salad with chips or tostadas, or as a party snack.

new nicoise salad

serves 4

prep: 30 minutes / cook: 30 minutes

THIS TWIST ON A TRADITIONAL NICOISE SALAD BRINGS PASTA INTO THE MIX and skips the anchovies.

SALAD:

½ cup orzo pasta

1 tablespoon olive oil

12 ounces baby lettuce

1 package (8 ounces) albacore tuna, drained, flaked

12 grape tomatoes, quartered

¾ pound sugar snap peas (cooked until crisp-tender, then cooled)

20 Nicoise olives

1 cucumber, halved, sliced

DRESSING:

2 cloves garlic, minced

¼ cup fresh lemon juice

¼ teaspoon salt

6 tablespoons olive oil

Fresh basil, julienned

① Cook the pasta; drain. Rinse until cool; toss with the 1 tablespoon olive oil.

② Divide the lettuce among 4 plates. Divide the tuna among the plates and add the grape tomatoes, sugar snap peas, olives and cucumber.

③ In a bowl, whisk together the garlic, lemon juice and salt. Slowly whisk in the 6 tablespoons olive oil.

④ Drizzle the dressing over the salad. Sprinkle with the fresh basil. Serve.

spinach and fingerling potato salad with warm bacon dressing

serves 6

prep: 15 minutes / cook: 15 minutes

WARM VINAIGRETTE DRESSING, SPIKED WITH CRUMBLED BACON, IS A CLAS-sic for potato or spinach salads. For this recipe, developed in the Tribune test kitchen, we combine the two salads, enhancing the idea with the bright flavor of orange zest and the crunch of toasted pine nuts.

½ pound each: fingerling potatoes, thick-cut bacon

2 large shallots, minced

½ cup olive oil

¼ cup red wine vinegar

2 tablespoons maple syrup

2 teaspoons minced orange zest

½ teaspoon each: salt, freshly ground pepper

½ pound baby spinach

½ cup pine nuts, toasted, see note

① Heat a large pot of salted water to a boil; add potatoes. Cook until potatoes are tender, 10–15 minutes. Drain; let cool until just warm. Cut into ¼-inch slices; set aside.

② Cook bacon in a skillet over medium-low heat until crisp but still chewy, 8 minutes. Drain bacon on paper towels. Let cool. Chop or crumble into bits; set aside. Pour all but 1 tablespoon fat from skillet; wipe clean. Turn heat to medium-high. Cook shallots until golden, 1 minute.

③ Mix bacon, oil, shallots, vinegar, maple syrup and orange zest in a small bowl. Season with salt and pepper. Heat in microwave until warm, about 30 seconds. Toss potatoes and spinach in large bowl with dressing. Garnish with pine nuts.

NOTE: To toast pine nuts, place in a dry skillet over medium-low heat. Cook, stirring nuts occasionally, until golden brown, 1–2 minutes. Watch carefully to avoid burning.

how to cook bacon perfectly

Slice strips in half crosswise. Place in a large skillet over medium-low heat without crowding. If strips overlap they won't cook evenly.

☛ Turn bacon regularly as it cooks. Because pans have hot spots, move the strips around, switching ones in the middle with those on the outside. The bacon will take 5–10 minutes to cook, depending on the bacon, the pan and the heat.

☛ Just before you think the bacon has reached perfection, remove it and drain on paper towels. It will continue to cook a little as it sits.

☛ To control the sizzling grease you can use a spatter guard, sold at many cookware and department stores.

chioggia beet salad

serves 2
prep: 20 minutes

THIS RECIPE BY CHEF GEOFF RHYNE, FORMERLY OF SUGARTOAD IN NAPERVILLE, highlights the candy-striped Chioggia beet.

4 Chioggia beets, sliced

2 tangerines, 1 peeled and
   segmented, 1 for juice

1 shallot

Olive oil

¼ cup sunflower sprouts

Fresh goat cheese

① Toss beets, tangerine segments and shallot. Drizzle with tangerine juice and olive oil. Sprinkle with sunflower sprouts. Crumble goat cheese atop.

beet carpaccio

serves 4

prep: 1 hour / cook: 40 minutes

ANTHONY MARTIN, EXECUTIVE CHEF/PARTNER OF CHICAGO'S TRU RESTAUrant, stresses this is a dish one can most definitely make at home, even if that means subbing goat cheese for the caviar and arugula for the greenery. Still, try for the caviar if you can. Martin, who created this dish especially for the Tribune, likes the pairing of sweet "earthiness" of the baby beet with the "soft nuttiness" of caviar. The beet has a presence, he adds, but still allows the caviar to shine. Martin uses a domestically sourced osetra caviar—and he likes to use enough of it to make an impression. Martin quickly arranges the thinly-sliced beets in concentric circles on the plate, each thin petal slightly overlapping its neighbor. Using tweezers, he carefully lays individual sprigs of fern-like chervil outside the outer ring of red beets. He spoons on the caviar and uses a teeny-tiny melon baller to scoop out equally tiny balls of green apple. A small pastry tube is used to squeeze dots of creme fraiche flavored with horseradish at strategic points. "Keep it natural," Martin says as he builds the beet carpaccio presentation, working toward a symmetry that's pleasing to the eye but not forced or too rigid.

BEETS:

4 each: baby Red Ace beets, baby candy strip beets, baby golden beets

2 tablespoons plus 2 teaspoons olive oil

1½ teaspoons sherry vinegar

1 ¼ teaspoons salt

APPLE GARNISH:

1 Granny Smith apple

1 teaspoon olive oil

¼ teaspoon lemon juice

⅛ teaspoon salt

CREME FRAICHE:

2 ounces creme fraiche

¼ teaspoon prepared horseradish

⅛ teaspoon salt or to taste

GARNISHES:

Caviar

Chervil

Allium or chive blossoms

Chive

continued

beet carpaccio

(continued)

① Toss clean unpeeled beets in a mixing bowl with 1 tablespoon plus 2 teaspoons olive oil and 1 teaspoon salt. Make three squares of aluminum foil that are about 10 inches on each side.

② Separate the beets according to color and place them on the foil squares. Wrap the beets in the foil. Place the foil packages on a sheet tray and bake the beets in a 350-degree oven for approximately 40 minutes, or until soft.

③ Leave the beets wrapped in foil and let sit until cool enough to handle. Open the packages and remove the skin.

④ Slice the beets into ⅛-inch rounds. Keep the colors separated. Place the three colors of sliced beets into three separate bowls, being careful not to break them. Drizzle each bowl of beets with a teaspoon of olive oil, ½ teaspoon sherry vinegar and a pinch of salt.

⑤ For the apple garnish, using a very small melon baller, make several small balls out of the apple. Alternatively, dice the apple into ¼-inch cubes. Place in a bowl; season with olive oil, lemon and salt.

⑥ For the creme fraiche, place the creme fraiche in a small bowl, incorporate the horseradish and season with salt. Pour into a small pastry tube or squeeze bottle.

⑦ When ready to serve, plate the beets in concentric circles by color. Start with the outside red ring, then a ring of candy stripe beets and, in the center, a golden beet.

⑧ Dot with the creme fraiche, decorate with the various garnishes.

why this salad is great

☛ **BEETS** – They add earthiness and an instant blast of color. Martin chose three varieties of beets for their flavor and color: golden, candy stripe (aka Chioggia) and Red Ace.

☛ **CAVIAR** – Go a little bigger than you think you should. Martin uses a domestically sourced osetra caviar—and he likes to use about ¼ to ½ teaspoon of roe per dollop. For a twist, try a wasabi-seasoned tobiko, the flying fish roe used in sushi.

☛ **GARNISHES** – They make the dish: Allium flowers and chervil sprigs were used to decorate the plate. Martin suggests substituting arugula for the chervil and the blossoms if needed. Don't have a really tiny melon baller for the apple? No problem; just cut into small cubes, the chef says.

EASY-TO-PACK MAIN DISHES

shrimp sandwiches with chili mayonnaise p. 122

« tuna sandwich p. 124

grilled english cheddar sandwich with smoked bacon and apple p. 126

angie johnson's pasties p. 127

torta americana p. 129

tofu po' boy p. 131

better than BLTs p. 132

medianoche p. 134

baja fish tacos p. 137

ethiopian chicken wraps p. 140

mackerel, carrot & herb salad sandwiches p. 143

chicken salad sandwich p. 144

shrimp sandwiches with chili mayonnaise

makes 4 sandwiches
prep: 20 minutes

I F YOU CAN FIND A BRIOCHE LOAF FOR THIS SIMPLE SUMMER SANDWICH, ALL THE better, but it's dreamy on plain white toast too. And it's so fast, it will make you feel spoiled. In fact, it's the kind of white-toast sandwich that ladies-who-lunch might order at the lunch counter at an upscale department store if ladies-who-lunch still ate white-toast sandwiches at upscale department store lunch counters. Maybe they do. If so, here's to the ladies who lunch.

1 cup mayonnaise

2 tablespoons minced red onion

1 tablespoon lemon or lime juice

2 teaspoons bottled red chili sauce (such as sriracha) or to taste

8 slices white bread or brioche, toasted

1 pound large cooked cleaned shrimp, sliced lengthwise

1 small bunch arugula

1 large ripe avocado, sliced

① Whisk together the mayonnaise, red onion, lemon juice and chili sauce in a small bowl.

② Spread half of the toast slices with 1 tablespoon chili mayonnaise each, or to taste; layer with shrimp, arugula leaves, then avocado. Top with remaining slices of toast; press lightly with palm of hand. Slice on diagonal.

TIPS

☛ Serve the leftover chili mayonnaise with cold slices of poached chicken, or use it in a chicken or egg salad.

☛ We used the Thai chili sauce sriracha, but you can also use Tabasco or your favorite chili sauce.

tuna sandwich

serves 4

prep: 30 minutes / grill: 10 minutes

pictured on p. 120

FISH TAKES NATURALLY TO THE GRILL. IT MUST BE THE CONTRAST BETWEEN water and fire, cool and hot, brine and char. Or the affinity between summer and easy. Rightfully, they go together.

Fish + grill can also = terrible. It must be the proximity of frying pan and fire. Overdone and undergood. Burned and "can we order pizza?" You can't go wrong with the tuna fish sandwich. Especially if you hike upscale—grilling fresh tuna, crisping fresh bread and seasoning with fresh herbs. It's a fresh approach to an old favorite, proving that the pairing of fish and 'wich never flops.

1¼ pounds fresh tuna steak, about 1 inch thick

2 tablespoons olive oil, plus more for skillet

2 tablespoons lemon juice

Coarse salt

Freshly ground pepper

Fresh thyme leaves

1 clove garlic, peeled, whole

8 slices country-style (or Italian) bread

Quickie aioli, recipe follows

Capers

Tomatoes sliced and sprinkled with coarse salt

Red onion, thinly sliced

Fresh dill, tough stems removed

① Drizzle tuna with 2 tablespoons olive oil and lemon juice. Season generously with salt, pepper and thyme. Let rest at room temperature, turning once, 15 minutes.

② Heat a thin film of olive oil in a heavy skillet. Add garlic clove, let sizzle 2 minutes; discard garlic. Add bread, in batches, and crisp golden, about 2 minutes per side, adding more oil as needed. Set 2 slices bread on each of 4 plates.

③ Prepare a medium-hot grill. Sizzle tuna until nicely browned outside and still rosy inside, about 4 minutes per side.

④ Slice tuna ¼-inch thick. Spread bread with aioli. Sprinkle on a few capers. Fan out tuna slices on 4 bread slices, dividing equally. Layer on tomato, onion and dill. Top each sandwich with a second slice of bread. Enjoy.

quickie aioli

serves 8
prep: 5 minutes

½ cup mayonnaise

1 tablespoon lemon juice

½ tablespoon olive oil

1 crushed clove garlic

① In a bowl, whisk together the mayonnaise, lemon juice, olive oil and garlic.

grilled english cheddar sandwich with smoked bacon and apple

serves 4
prep: 15 minutes / cook: 12 minutes

To capture the authentic flavor of this sandwich, adapted from Artisanal restaurant in New York City, use a sharp Cheddar cheese such as the Keen or Montgomery brands from Somerset, England, a smoky bacon such as Nueske's from Wisconsin, and traditional French pain au levain, a sourdough-style bread. Otherwise, make substitutions as needed.

8 slices thick-cut, applewood-smoked bacon

8 slices sourdough country-style bread

16 thin slices sharp Cheddar cheese, about ½ pound

1 large Granny Smith apple, quartered, cored, cut into 16 slices

1 teaspoon ground red pepper or to taste

4 tablespoons butter, melted

① Cut bacon slices in half; place in a large skillet over low heat. Cook until crisp but still flexible, about 6 minutes. Place on paper towels to drain. Discard fat from skillet; wipe clean with paper towel.

② Top 4 slices of the bread with 2 slices of the cheese, 4 of the apple slices, ¼ teaspoon of the red pepper, bacon and 2 more slices of the cheese. Cover with remaining bread slices. Brush the outside of each bread slice with melted butter.

③ Heat the skillet over medium heat. Place the sandwiches butter side down in the skillet. Butter tops of sandwiches. Cook until browned on one side, about 3 minutes. Turn; cook other side 3 minutes. Remove to a cutting board; press down with a spatula before serving.

angie johnson's pasties

makes 6 pasties

prep: 35 minutes / chill: 15 minutes / cook: 15 minutes

IT HAS BEEN SAID THAT "A MINE IS A HOLE IN THE GROUND WITH A CORNISHMAN at the bottom," to which might be added "and a pasty." That's because the Cornish miners who came to the Upper Peninsula of Michigan more than 100 years ago brought not only their mining skills but also their favorite dish. Most of the mines are closed now, but pasties—those rich, flaky pastries filled with meat and vegetables—are still popular in the North Woods. Almost every town in the Upper Peninsula has at least one pasty shop, and each shop usually has a traditional recipe, one used by a grandmother or great-aunt, that has been in the family for generations. The recipes hardly vary. "I learned how to make them more than 65 years ago," says Angie Johnson, a great grandmother who lives in Iron Mountain, Mich. Johnson says that to save time some of her friends use store-bought pie crust.

3 cups flour	1 small each, finely chopped: onion, peeled rutabaga, potato
1 teaspoon salt	
1 cup shortening	1 pound ground round
½ cup cold water	1 large egg mixed with 1 tablespoon water
1 tablespoon butter	

① Combine flour and salt in large bowl. Cut in shortening with pastry blender or 2 knives. Slowly add water until dough forms. Cover; refrigerate 15 to 20 minutes.

② Melt butter in medium skillet over medium heat. Add onion; cook, stirring often, until soft, about 4 minutes. Add rutabaga and potato; cook until tender, about 4 minutes. Add ground round; cook until meat is no longer pink. Drain fat. Set aside to cool.

③ Heat oven to 400 degrees. Divide dough into 6 equal pieces; roll each piece into 8-inch circle on floured work surface. Place 1 cup of filling on half of each circle; spread to about ¼-inch from edge. Brush edges with egg-water mixture. Fold unfilled side over to form semicircle, pressing down on edges to seal. Crimp edges. Brush tops with egg-water mixture. Repeat with remaining dough.

④ Place pasties on greased baking sheet. Bake until pasties are golden brown, about 15 minutes.

torta americana

serves 4
prep: 10 minutes

AMERICANS ARE FAMILIAR WITH USING TORTILLAS TO MAKE WRAPPED AND rolled sandwiches. But our favorite Mexican sandwich is the torta, made on crusty rolls called bollillos. "They're so simple, we eat them all the time in Mexico," said Priscila Satkoff, chef/co-owner of Salpicon. She inspired this version.

- 4 crusty dinner rolls or 2 medium baguettes
- 1 cup refried black beans
- 4 ounces crumbled queso fresco (Mexican white cheese)
- 8 ounces sliced ham
- ¼ cup chopped cilantro
- 2 limes, halved
- ¼ cup each: salsa, sour cream, optional

① Split the dinner rolls in half lengthwise. If using baguettes, cut them in half, then split each half lengthwise.

② Spread each roll with refried black beans; sprinkle the queso fresco equally over the halves. Top with ham; sprinkle with cilantro. Drizzle each half with lime juice.

③ Press the sandwiches lightly with your hands to flatten a little. Serve sandwiches with sour cream and salsa as a dressing, if desired.

tofu po' boy

serves 4

prep: 20 minutes / marinate: 1 hour / cook: 20 minutes

Po' BOY SANDWICHES HAVE A LONG, RICH HERITAGE. THIS VEGAN VERSION OF the classic sandwich is adapted from Mark Shadle, owner of G-Zen restaurant in Branford, Conn.

1 pound extra-firm tofu	½ teaspoon crushed black pepper
½ cup white wine	1 long baguette or 4 small baguettes
¼ cup soy sauce	
1 tablespoon toasted sesame oil	1 to 2 cups kimchee
1 tablespoon fresh basil, minced (or 1 teaspoon dried)	Sriracha sauce
	Sliced tomatoes and fresh basil leaves

① Place tofu between two plates; weight with a heavy can. Let rest in sink, 1 hour. Pour off exuded water. Slice block into 4 pieces. Mix wine, soy sauce, sesame oil, basil and black pepper in a small bowl. Pour marinade over tofu; let stand, 1 hour or up to 24 hours.

② Place tofu pieces and the marinade in a baking dish; bake in a 400-degree oven, 10 minutes. Turn tofu pieces over; bake, 5 minutes. Remove tofu from oven; allow to cool.

③ Cut long baguette into four 4-inch lengths or use individual baguettes; slice the bread open lengthwise. Pull some of the bread out to create a shallow well to hold the filling.

④ Reheat tofu on a hot grill, to create grill marks and heat through, no more than 5 minutes. Place tofu in baguettes. Top with kimchee; drizzle with sriracha sauce. Garnish with tomato and basil.

better than BLTs

serves 4

prep: 15 minutes / cook: 10 minutes

"THE KEY TO A GREAT BLT IS THE BREAD, AND THE QUALITY INGREDIENTS," says Carol Watson of Milk and Honey Cafe. "I like to use pane francese from Red Hen bread. Our BLT at the cafe is a triple-decker. We drizzle the bread with extra-virgin olive oil and toast both sides on our grill." Here's our interpretation of her idea.

½ cup mayonnaise

¼ cup minced fresh basil

2 cloves garlic, minced

8 slices sturdy rustic bread

1 tablespoon extra-virgin olive oil

½ pound pancetta, coarsely diced

8 ounces baby arugula or baby lettuce

4 plum tomatoes, thinly sliced lengthwise

½ pound fresh mozzarella, sliced

① Stir the mayonnaise, basil and garlic together in a small bowl until well combined; set aside.

② Heat the broiler. Place the bread slices on a baking sheet; brush lightly with olive oil on both sides. Broil, turning once, to toast; set aside.

③ Heat a medium skillet over medium heat. Add the pancetta; cook, stirring often, until the pancetta is crisp and browned, about 3 minutes each side. Transfer to a paper towel to drain.

④ Place 4 slices of the toasted bread on each of 4 plates. Spread each with the mayonnaise mixture. Divide the arugula among the 4 slices. Layer tomatoes and mozzarella on the bread. Top each sandwich with remaining slices of the bread.

medianoche

serves 4

prep: 10 minutes

THIS IS CALLED A "MIDNIGHT SANDWICH," SAID MAYRA FERNANDEZ OF CAFE Cubano, "because you go into the fridge to get something to eat late at night." Fernandez recommends using faintly sweetened egg bread for an authentic flavor. An authentic medianoche sandwich would be grilled, but to save time and effort, our version is simply assembled and pressed briefly.

8 slices egg bread, such as challah or Cuban bread

2 tablespoons each: mayonnaise, mustard

4 slices each: ham, turkey, Swiss cheese

4 dill pickles, thinly sliced lengthwise

① Spread the sliced bread with mayonnaise and mustard. Layer ham, turkey, cheese and dill pickles on bottom slices of bread; top with remaining slices.

② Wrap the sandwiches in foil or plastic wrap; press sandwiches using your hands or a heavy skillet.

fish tacos locos (above left, p. 153) and baja fish tacos (above right, p. 137)

baja fish tacos

serves 4
prep: 20 minutes / cook: 10 minutes

FISH TACOS BEGAN LIFE AS AFTER-WORK SUSTENANCE FOR FISHERMEN IN Ensenada, Mexico, became cool as the snack of choice for surfers and their pals in the Baja Peninsula and have now circled the globe as a trendy bar nosh and alternative to the shrimp cocktail. The original fish taco was a humble scrap of the catch of the day, battered and fried by fishmongers on the pier or at the fish market, dressed with crunchy cabbage, creamy sauce, a dab of salsa and a squeeze of lime, all nestled in a corn tortilla or two for easy eating. Simple. Fresh. Delicious. Don't forget a big bowl of fresh lime wedges for the fresh finishing squirt.

¾ cup flour

¼ cup cornmeal

1 teaspoon salt

¼ teaspoon cayenne pepper

1 cup beer (Mexican lager is most authentic)

Oil for frying

1 pound firm-fleshed fish fillets like cod or halibut, cut into thick strips or cubes

Salsa fresca, recipe follows

Creamy cabbage slaw, recipe follows

1 dozen corn tortillas, warmed

4 limes, cut into wedges

① Combine flour, cornmeal, salt and cayenne in a large mixing bowl. Stir in beer until the mixture is smooth.

② Heat 2–3 inches of oil in a cast-iron skillet to 375 degrees. Dip each piece of fish in beer batter; add to oil, being careful to avoid crowding. Fry until golden, turning if necessary. Remove from oil; transfer to a tray lined with paper towels. Season lightly with salt; serve at once with salsa, slaw, warm tortillas and lime.

salsa fresca

prep: 20 minutes / chill: 30–60 minutes

CHOOSE A TRADITIONAL PICO DE GALLO BY USING FRESH TOMATOES, OR GO loco by adding fresh fruit or vegetables.

2 cups chopped ripe tomatoes (or 2 cups any combination of chopped tomatillos, pineapple, mango, jicama, melon, berries, corn and/ or cucumber)

½ small red onion, chopped

1 jalapeno, minced

3 tablespoons fresh lime juice

¼ cup chopped fresh cilantro

Salt and pepper to taste

① Combine all ingredients in a bowl.

② Allow to sit 30–60 minutes refrigerated before serving.

creamy cabbage slaw

prep: 15 minutes
stand: slaw is best when allowed to sit overnight in the fridge to soften the cabbage, but it can be served right away.

BY ADDING THE TRADITIONAL CREAMY DRESSING DIRECTLY TO THE SLAW, YOU make taco assembly less messy.

1 head green or red cabbage, shredded

¼ cup green onions, sliced

¼ cup cider vinegar

1 teaspoon salt

1 cup mayonnaise

1 cup sour cream, yogurt or creme fraiche

1 tablespoon chopped chipotles in adobo, optional

① Combine all ingredients in a large bowl.

② Refrigerate overnight or serve right away.

ethiopian chicken wraps

serves 6

prep: 30 minutes / rise: 30 minutes / cook: 50 minutes / stand: 10 minutes

I NJERA IS THE SPONGY, SLIGHTLY SOUR ETHIOPIAN FLATBREAD THAT SERVES AS plate, utensil and tablecloth in Ethiopian homes. It's easy enough to make—like pancakes that don't need to be flipped. Authentic injera is made from teff, a grain ground into flour. This more accessible version, adapted from Dorinda Hafner's "A Taste of Africa," uses readily available ingredients. We've also adapted Hafner's small-quantity mixture for the spicy-hot seasoning mix called berbere.

BREAD:

1 cup self-rising flour

¾ teaspoon active dry yeast

2 cups plus 2 tablespoons lukewarm water

BERBERE:

3 tablespoons ground red pepper

1 tablespoon sweet paprika

½ teaspoon each: salt, ground ginger

¼ teaspoon ground cinnamon

⅛ teaspoon ground dried mint

FILLING:

1 tablespoon vegetable oil

2 boneless, skinless chicken breast halves

2 large yellow onions, sliced

① Heat a large skillet over medium-low heat; add the flour to the dry skillet. Cook the flour until dark brown, stirring continuously to prevent burning, about 10 minutes. Transfer the flour to a large bowl; set aside to cool slightly, about 5 minutes.

② Soak the yeast in ¼ cup of the lukewarm water; let stand until it is foamy, about 10 minutes. Stir to completely dissolve yeast. Stir into the flour and add remaining lukewarm water. Cover the batter with a dish towel; let rest 30 minutes.

③ Heat a large nonstick skillet over medium heat. Stir the batter well; ladle about ¼ cup of the batter into the skillet. Swirl the batter around the skillet to completely cover the bottom of the skillet, as if making one big pancake. Cook until pale caramel, using a spatula to gently lift the edges to check the doneness, about 5–7 minutes. Transfer to a baking sheet lined with wax paper. Repeat with the remaining batter.

④ For the berbere, combine red pepper, paprika, salt, ginger, cinnamon and mint in a small bowl. Rub the chicken breasts with the berbere. Heat oil in a large skillet over medium heat. Add the chicken; cook, turning once, until cooked through and browned, about 15 minutes. Transfer the chicken to a cutting board. Add the onion to the skillet; cook, stirring occasionally, until the onion is softened and golden, about 6 minutes.

⑤ Meanwhile, shred the chicken using two forks or your fingers. Spread one-sixth of the chicken over the bottom third of an injera; top with one-sixth of the onions. Season with additional berbere if you wish. Roll the bottom third of the injera up to cover the chicken mixture; fold in each side. Roll the injera like a burrito.

mackerel, carrot & herb salad sandwiches

makes 2 sandwiches

prep: 15 minutes / stand: 8–10 minutes

THIS RECIPE IS A DELICIOUSLY ELEVATED BASIC BY LYDIA ESPARZA AND NICK Lessins of famed (and now shuttered) Great Lake pizza.

1 can mackerel

1 cup thinly sliced carrots

1 cup coarsely chopped flat-leaf parsley

2 teaspoons minced sweet onion

1 tablespoon Dijon mustard

4 teaspoons mayonnaise

Freshly ground pepper and sea salt to taste

4 slices rustic bakery bread, toasted

Fresh spinach leaves

① Combine mackerel with its oil, carrots, parsley and onion in a bowl; mix in Dijon mustard and mayonnaise. Season with freshly ground pepper and sea salt, if needed. Let stand.

② Scoop the salad onto the bread. Top with fresh spinach leaves.

chicken salad sandwich

serves 2
prep: 20 minutes

PICK THIS FOR YOUR NEXT PICNIC: CHEF MERLIN VERRIER'S CHICKEN SALAD sandwich with herb aioli. Save time with a rotisserie chicken from the grocery store.

8 ounces cooked chicken

¼ cup each: sliced red grapes, small-diced red onion, small-diced celery, Italian parsley, chopped

1 tablespoon fresh tarragon, chopped

2 tablespoons herb aioli, see recipe

4 slices mixed grain bread

1 tablespoon blue cheese crumbles

1 tablespoon chopped walnuts

Handful mixed greens

① Shred the chicken and mix in grapes, onion, celery, parsley, tarragon and herb aioli.

② Top two slices of bread with the salad. Top with blue cheese crumbles, walnuts, greens and remaining bread slices.

---

herb aioli

makes 1 cup
prep: 10 minutes

½ cup mayonnaise

1 tablespoon Dijon

1 tablespoon white wine vinegar or Champagne vinegar

½ teaspoon Tabasco

¼ cup each: parsley and tarragon (both lightly packed)

1 teaspoon minced garlic

1 tablespoon chopped red onion

① Puree all ingredients in a blender.

summer's best main dishes

GRILLED AND SLOW-COOKED DELIGHTS

grilled tomato and olive pizza p. 148

grilled eggplant p. 150

grilled veggies p. 152

fish tacos locos p. 153

jerk chicken pinchos p. 154

BBQ chicken p. 156

simple summer chicken p. 159

caribbean-style garlic-soaked shrimp p. 160

grilled branzino with smoked salt and pepper p. 163

grilled octopus salad with grapefruit balsamic vinegar p. 164

grilled shrimp with sambal p. 167

carne asada with chimichurri p. 169

chorizo burgers with queso fresco p. 171

bacon, turkey and beef burgers p. 172

« flank steak 4 ways p. 173

butterflied leg of lamb p. 181

slow lemon brisket p. 182

low country boil p. 185

michigan baked beans p. 187

green chili with chicken p. 188

grilled tomato and olive pizza

serves 3

prep: 20 minutes / cook: 15 minutes

WHEN EVERYONE HAD A CHANCE TO ADD FAVORITE INGREDIENTS FOR MADE-to-order pizzas, the Tribune's Donna Pierce chose one of her favorite late-summer combinations: tomatoes and olives. Here's a tip: Shop the supermarket salad bar for topping suggestions...with pizza, everything goes.

½ pint cocktail or grape tomatoes, halved

½ red onion, thinly sliced

¼ cup olive oil

3 tablespoons each: pitted kalamata olives, drained, chopped sun-dried tomatoes

½ teaspoon salt

Freshly ground pepper

1 package unbaked pizza dough, stretched into 12-inch round, or prepared (12-inch) pizza crust, see note

2 tablespoons chopped fresh parsley

¼ to ½ cup shredded fontina

2 tablespoons each: torn basil leaves, shredded Parmesan

① Heat a grill to high. Combine the tomatoes, onion, 3 tablespoons of the olive oil, olives, sun-dried tomatoes, salt and pepper to taste in a bowl, tossing to coat with your hands. Brush the remaining 1 tablespoon of the olive oil over both sides of the pizza crust.

② Place the dough over direct heat on grill; cook until puffy, about 2 minutes; turn over. Cook 2 minutes. Move crust to a cooler part of the grill; top with the tomato-olive mixture. Sprinkle the parsley, fontina and basil over the top. Cover grill; cook until cheese melts, about 8 minutes. Sprinkle with Parmesan. Cover; cook until cheese melts, about 2 minutes. Remove from grill; cut into wedges.

NOTE: If you are using a prepared crust, follow directions on the package for cooking instructions.

grilled eggplant

serves 4

prep: 35 minutes / cook: 5 minutes

THE VEGETABLE, NO MATTER HOW EMBARRASSINGLY AMPLE, NEED NOT BE RE-pressed under a smooth layer of bechamel, shoved to the margins of the plate or coaxed into some meat-substitute masquerade. We prefer an honest approach. Served in plain sight, to consenting adults, without apology. There's no reason eggplant, grilled smoky and glowing with garlic, can't command a meal in itself. Unless, of course, you've already indulged in the same for breakfast and lunch. All week. Too much of a good thing is, it turns out, an attainable condition.

SAUCE:

2 tablespoons minced garlic

1 tablespoon minced ginger

⅓ packed cup cilantro leaves and stems

½ cup unsalted peanut butter

½ cup soy sauce

¼ cup sugar

1 teaspoon rice vinegar

1 tablespoon hot chili oil

VEGETABLES:

4 to 6 long Asian eggplants (standard eggplants, though thicker-skinned and not as sweet, work too)

½ cup sesame oil

① Measure all the sauce ingredients into the food processor. Swirl smooth.

② Halve the eggplants lengthwise. Score the flesh lightly with crisscross hatch marks. Brush the cut sides liberally with sesame oil. Lay them, cut sides down, on a baking sheet.

③ Prepare a medium-hot grill. Grill eggplants, cut sides down, until golden and striped with score marks and the thickest portion of the skin side is tender to the touch, about 5 minutes.

④ Cut the eggplant halves on the diagonal and arrange, scored sides up, on a plate. Spoon on the sauce. Enjoy hot or warm, accompanied by a wedge of crispy noodle pillow (recipe follows).

crispy noodle pillow

serves 4

prep: 20 minutes / cook: 30 minutes

½ pound wide lo mein noodles

2 tablespoons finely chopped chives (Chinese or standard)

2 tablespoons thinly sliced scallions

2 teaspoons sesame oil

½ teaspoon coarse salt

Freshly ground black pepper

3 tablespoons corn oil

① Cook the noodles to al dente. Drain, rinse with cold water, drain again.

② Toss the noodles with the chives, scallions, sesame oil, salt and black pepper.

③ Heat the corn oil in a medium nonstick skillet over medium heat. Coil the noodles into the skillet and press even with a spatula. Cook until golden on one side, about 7 minutes. Flip and cook until golden on the other side, about 8 minutes more.

④ Slide onto a baking sheet lined with paper towels. Cut into wedges, which are handy for catching stray peanut sauce.

grilled veggies

serves 4

prep time: 30 minutes / cook time: 35 minutes

Oh, this recipe, adapted from one by Donna Pierce, would be a treat indeed to pair with wines, white and red, equally aromatic and juicy of flavor. Shy not from red wines with all-vegetable dishes; many fit, especially if the food has fat (this does) and the wine has tannin (most reds do). Pinot noir, barbera, some Chianti, there's the ticket. Just avoid alcoholic (15 percent and above) and tannic, blockbuster reds such as, say, Napa cabernet. They have their place, but it isn't here. They're just too, well, meaty.

2 small eggplants, cut in 1-inch chunks

2 zucchini, thinly sliced

2 red onions, thinly sliced

1 yellow onion, thinly sliced

8 ounces sliced mushrooms

2 tablespoons olive oil

Salt to taste

2 tomatoes, diced

¼ cup pitted olives, halved

Crumbled goat cheese for serving

① Prepare a medium hot grill.

② In a large bowl, combine eggplants, zucchini, onions and mushrooms; toss with 2 tablespoons olive oil and salt to taste. Place vegetables on a large piece of foil with edges folded up.

③ Transfer vegetables to a hot grill. Cover; cook, 20 minutes. Stir in tomatoes. Cook until vegetables are tender.

④ Carefully slide a cookie sheet under the foil to remove vegetables from grill. Add olives. Serve with crumbled goat cheese.

fish tacos locos

serves 4
prep: 15 minutes / cook: 6–10 minutes
pictured on p. 136

FISH TACOS MAKE A GREAT CHOICE AS PART OF A FESTIVE BUT LAID-BACK LABOR Day menu. Grill some spiced-up fish steaks (halibut or swordfish are perfect choices) and serve with a creamy slaw (Jason McLeod, a chef in San Diego who has downed many a taco, recommends adding tangy creme fraiche to the dressing), salsa fresca from a jar or from this season's harvest, and a pile of corn tortillas for a make-your-own taco bar.

¼ cup blackening seasoning mix

1½ pounds fish steaks, such as halibut, mahi-mahi, swordfish or tuna

Salsa fresca (see p. 138)

Creamy cabbage slaw, (see p. 138)

1 dozen corn tortillas, warmed

4 limes, cut into wedges

① Prepare a grill for medium-high heat.

② Spread the seasoning mix on a plate; dip in the fish steaks, pressing slightly to adhere. Grill the steaks on each side until well-browned and cooked through, about 3–5 minutes per side.

③ Serve with salsa, slaw, tortillas and lime wedges.

jerk chicken pinchos

serves 6

prep: 30 minutes / grill: 10 minutes

PINCHO IS SPANISH FOR SKEWER. MUCH LIKE THE FRENCH BROCHETTE, THE Middle Eastern kebab or the rustic whittled stick, the pincho skewers chunks of pineapple and jerk chicken—the allspice-rubbed, charcoal-grilled Jamaican street staple. Drizzled with cilantro salsa and dusted with Mexican cheese, this recipe, adapted from chef Jorge Pimentel of Sabor'a Street food truck in Washington, D.C., tours many a sunny destination, on wheels.

2 tablespoons plus ½ teaspoon coarse salt

2 tablespoons brown sugar

2 tablespoons finely chopped garlic

2 tablespoons allspice

1 tablespoon plus ½ teaspoon ground black pepper

1 tablespoon red pepper flakes

1 tablespoon ground ginger

½ tablespoon thyme (fresh or dried)

4 whole (1-pound) boneless, skinless chicken breasts, cut into 1½-inch cubes

1 whole pineapple, peeled, cored, cut into 1½-inch cubes

8 ounces queso fresco, grated

Salsa verde, recipe follows

① Make jerk seasoning by combining 2 tablespoons salt, sugar, garlic, allspice, 1 tablespoon black pepper, red pepper, ginger and thyme in a large bowl. Add chicken and toss to coat. Let rest 15 minutes. In a separate bowl toss pineapple with ½ teaspoon salt and ½ teaspoon pepper.

② Soak bamboo skewers in water at least 10 minutes (or use metal skewers). Thread chicken and pineapple onto skewers, starting and ending with pineapple chunks.

③ Grill directly over medium heat until chicken is cooked through, about 10 minutes.

④ Top each skewer with salsa verde and shredded cheese. For authentic food-truck style, enjoy standing on the sidewalk.

salsa verde

serves 6
prep: 10 minutes

2 cloves whole garlic
1 bunch cilantro
1 tablespoon apple cider vinegar

1 teaspoon coarse salt
1 teaspoon freshly ground black pepper
¼ cup canola (or other mild) oil

① Drop the garlic cloves into a running food processor. Buzz to bits. Add leaves and tender stems from the cilantro, the apple cider vinegar, the salt and the black pepper. Pulse to a rough sauce. With machine running, pour in the oil to make a thick sauce.

BBQ chicken

serves 4–6

prep: 20 minutes / wait: 3 or more hours / grill: 25 minutes

L EAH ESKIN REMEMBERS: "SUMMERS, DAD WOULD BARBECUE CHICKEN. PROB-ably also sausage and steak and—later on—veggie burgers for the nonconformist teen, but what sticks in memory is chicken. I didn't like it. I liked the idea of it—of chicken sauced sticky and grilled crispy and seared sticky-crispy, best pressed directly onto a sticky-crispy face while standing barefoot in the grass, in a swimsuit, near the sprinkler. What we got was this: burnt. Maybe the adults considered it singed, flambe or well-done but I, age 6 and opinionated, knew it was burnt.

Face to face with leaping flame and dripping chicken I came to understand Dad's predicament: Chicken needs time to crisp. Sauce, given time, burns. The idea of saucing, then grilling, is flawed. I decided to separate the tasks, grilling first, saucing later and searing at the last minute. The technique worked. And it's delicious. Though I wish I had Dad around to burn it."

1 pound bone-in, skin-on drumsticks (about 5)	1 teaspoon coarse salt
3 pounds bone-in, skin-on split chicken breasts (each halved again—ask the butcher—to yield about 10 chunks)	½ teaspoon freshly ground black pepper
	Apricot barbecue sauce (recipe follows)

① Rinse and pat dry chicken. Rub salt and pepper into the chicken. Cover (or tumble into ziptop bags) and chill, 2 hours to 2 days. Let chicken come to room temperature, up to 1 hour, before grilling.

② Build (or spark) a medium-hot fire. Clean and lightly oil grates. Set chicken over flame and grill until golden outside and cooked through inside (165 degrees), about 12 minutes per side.

③ Brush chicken with sauce. Cook just long enough to sear sauce to chicken, about 1 minute per side. Enjoy, with napkins.

apricot barbecue sauce

serves 4–6

prep: 20 minutes / cook: 4 minutes

2 tablespoons each: soy sauce,
dry white wine or sherry, finely
chopped green onions, chopped
garlic, chopped fresh ginger,
lemon juice

½ cup apricot jam

¼ teaspoon red pepper flakes

① Combine the soy sauce, wine, green onions, garlic, ginger and lemon juice in the
food processor or blender. Add ½ cup apricot jam and ¼ teaspoon red pepper flakes.
Swirl smooth.

② Pour into a medium saucepan. Boil thick, stirring attentively, about 4 minutes.

simple summer chicken

serves 4

prep: 30 minutes / marinate: 5 minutes / grill: 26 minutes

WHEN THE SCENT OF SUMMER IS STILL IN SEASON, FARMER EMILY WETTSTEIN, of Carlock, Illinois, likes to marinate chicken in Italian dressing, then grill. Which works nicely. This version, in which the chicken is first grilled, then marinated, helps avoid flare-ups and allows the fresh lime and ginger to stand out.

¾ cup lime juice	2 teaspoons minced garlic
½ cup olive oil	1 3-pound chicken, quartered
1 tablespoon minced ginger	Salt, pepper
1 tablespoon sugar	

① Mix lime juice, olive oil, ginger, sugar and garlic in a large bowl. Set aside.

② Rinse chicken pieces and pat dry. Season with salt and pepper.

③ Grill the chicken directly over a medium-hot fire for 5 minutes on each side. Shift to indirect heat and continue cooking until done but moist, about another 8 minutes per side.

④ Move the chicken off the grill and into the bowl of marinade. Let the grilled chicken absorb the fragrant juice about 5 minutes. Serve warm.

caribbean-style garlic-soaked shrimp

serves 6

prep: 25 minutes / marinate: 30 minutes / cook: 4 minutes

I N CUBA, THE NATIVE SOUR ORANGE IS USED; HERE WE ADD LIME JUICE TO SIMU-late its flavor. This sauce is terrific on any seafood but is traditionally used for Cuban roast pork. The tropical flavors of the Caribbean suit our steamy summers. In our recipe for grilled shrimp al mojo, the marinade and the sauce are one and the same for easy execution and a powerful flavor punch that works on poultry or pork chops too. Serve with rice and black beans and a hearts of palm salad. Don't forget the mojitos.

½ cup fresh orange juice

¼ cup fresh lime juice

2 large cloves garlic, chopped

¼ cup extra-virgin olive oil

½ teaspoon each: kosher salt, freshly ground pepper

1½ pounds shrimp, peeled, deveined

½ cup sliced green onions

① Combine the juices, garlic, oil, salt and pepper in a large bowl. Reserve ½ cup in a separate container for serving; toss the shrimp in remaining marinade; marinate, refrigerated, 30 minutes to 2 hours.

② Heat grill to medium high. Thread the shrimp on skewers. Grill, turning once, until pink and firm, about 2 minutes per side. Place on a platter; drizzle with reserved sauce. Serve topped with green onions.

grilled branzino with smoked salt and pepper

serves 2

prep: 20 minutes / cook: 8–12 minutes

SMOKED SEA SALT AND BLACK PEPPER ADD A SMOKY DEPTH TO THIS MEDITER-ranean sea bass recipe by the Tribune's David Syrek.

2 whole branzino, cleaned
Smoked salt and freshly ground black pepper to taste

4 chopped leeks

1 large lemon, sliced, plus half-lemon, zested or sliced

2 tablespoons olive oil

Bay leaves for garnish

① Season the branzino cavity with the smoked salt and the pepper. Stuff with chopped leeks and lemon slices. Drizzle olive oil over the outside of the fish.

② Heat grill to medium heat. Grill fish until skin is crisp, about 4 to 6 minutes per side. Season with more smoked salt and pepper to taste.

③ Garnish with bay leaves and lemon zest or slices.

grilled octopus salad with grapefruit balsamic vinegar

serves 2–3
prep: 5 minutes / cook: 1 hour

THIS OCTOPUS SALAD WAS INSPIRED BY CHEF TAKASHI YAGIHASHI'S GRILLED octopus from Slurping Turtle and grapefruit white balsamic vinegar, a delightfully zingy vinegar with a lively, just-picked flavor. Grapefruit white balsamic vinegar can be found in artisan olive oil shops. Most octopi can be bought already cleaned.

2 pounds small octopus
  Sea salt and freshly ground pepper to taste
  Pinch of red pepper flakes

  Olive oil
1 head frisee lettuce
  Grapefruit white balsamic vinegar

① Place octopus and enough water to submerge in a pot over high heat and cover. Allow to boil about 10 minutes. Reduce heat to medium low and simmer about 45 minutes until octopus is tender.

② Remove from pot and season with sea salt, freshly ground pepper and a pinch of red pepper flakes. Drizzle with olive oil, coating the octopus.

③ Heat grill to medium high. Grill octopus directly over the fire until lightly charred (but not burnt), 2 to 4 minutes. Transfer to a board; cut into bite-size pieces, discarding heads.

④ Toss with lettuce; season with more salt and pepper to taste. Drizzle with olive oil and grapefruit white balsamic vinegar.

grilled shrimp with sambal

makes 16 shrimp

marinate: 1 hour / grill: 10 minutes

USE THIS SAMBAL, AN INDONESIAN CHILI SAUCE, AS THE FUEL TO SET YOUR tongue deliciously aflame. Chef Joncarl Lachman, formerly of the Dutch-accented Vincent restaurant in Chicago, uses sambal to spike up various dishes, from steamed mussels to grilled pork ribs. Indonesia is a former Dutch colony, and sambal—made from chili, sugar and salt in its simplest form—is a popular condiment in the Netherlands. Lachman plays up the spicy complexity of sambal by serving something simple, sweet and refreshing on the side. Watermelon works for Lachman, either sliced and served as is, or cubed into a salad. There are many forms of sambal available at grocery stores and Asian markets. The chef recommends home cooks buy the simplest blends so they can more easily customize the flavor as they're cooking.

1 cup sambal

½ cup soy sauce

¼ cup each: molasses, sugar

2 limes, juiced

10 cloves garlic

¼ cup olive oil

16 jumbo shrimp, head on

Garnishes: Grated ginger, lime zest, chopped cilantro

① In a blender, add sambal, soy sauce, molasses, sugar, lime juice, garlic and olive oil. Puree until smooth.

② Pour into a bowl with the shrimp and marinate 1 hour in refrigerator. In the meantime, heat grill to medium.

③ Skewer each shrimp. Grill about 10 minutes. Garnish with grated ginger, lime zest and chopped cilantro.

carne asada with chimichurri

serves 6

prep: 15 minutes / cook: 10 minutes

ARGENTINE COOKS ARE FAMOUS FOR THEIR SAVORY GRILLED MEATS, AND their signature chimichurri sauce accents carne asada perfectly. Make a big batch of this fresh green sauce and serve with grilled vegetables or seafood as well, for a less traditional but equally delicious idea. Try serving with a vinegar-based potato salad for a real change of pace, and pair it all with a malbec for authenticity. Fun fact: In Argentina, jugoso means rare, a punto means medium and cocido means well done.

1 cup flat-leaf parsley leaves (or ½ cup cilantro or basil plus ½ cup parsley)

2 tablespoons fresh oregano leaves

2 large cloves garlic, whole

¼ small yellow onion, whole

¼ cup extra-virgin olive oil

2 tablespoons red wine vinegar

½ teaspoon red chili flakes

Kosher salt and freshly ground pepper, to taste

2 pounds skirt steak or flank steak

① For chimichurri sauce, place all ingredients (except steak) into a blender; blend to a smooth sauce. Taste for seasoning.

② Heat grill to medium high. Season steak generously with kosher salt and freshly ground pepper. Place steak on grill; cook to desired doneness, turning once, 10 minutes. Allow to rest 5 minutes before slicing on the diagonal. Serve with chimichurri sauce, baguettes and a simple salad of lettuce, tomato, onion, oil and vinegar.

chorizo burgers with queso fresco

makes 8 burgers

prep: 30 minutes / chill: 2 hours or overnight / cook: 8–10 minutes

FOR MEAT LOVERS, MAKING MEXICAN-STYLE CHORIZO IS ALMOST EASIER THAN finding it at the grocery store. By grilling it in patties you skip the tricky steps of sausage-making, and can serve chorizo burgers with queso fresco and avocado salsa any day of the week. (Just remember to prepare the chorizo mixture a day ahead for better flavor.) Margaritas and chilled Mexican lager are a must.

3 to 4 tablespoons ancho chili powder
1 teaspoon kosher salt
2 large cloves garlic, finely chopped
2 teaspoons dried oregano, crumbled
1 teaspoon ground cinnamon
1 teaspoon ground cumin

1 teaspoon freshly ground pepper
¼ cup cider vinegar
2 pounds ground pork (or turkey, or a combination)
8 burger buns or bolillo rolls, toasted
8 ounces queso fresco, crumbled

① Combine chili powder, salt, garlic, oregano, cinnamon, cumin, pepper and vinegar in a large bowl. Add the meat; combine with your hands thoroughly. Form into 8 patties, wrap well in plastic and chill to blend flavors, at least 2 hours or overnight.

② Heat grill to medium high. Place patties on the grill; cook, turning once, until cooked through (internal temperature 155 degrees), about 3–4 minutes per side. Serve on toasted rolls topped with avocado salsa (recipe follows) and queso fresco.

avocado salsa

makes 4 cups

prep: 25 minutes

2 large ripe avocados, diced
1 large tomato or 8 tomatillos, diced
1 jalapeno, diced, optional
Juice of 4 limes

½ red onion, chopped finely
1 clove garlic, chopped
½ cup chopped fresh cilantro
¼ to ½ teaspoon kosher salt

① Combine all ingredients in a bowl; stir gently without smashing. Salsa should be chunky. Taste for seasoning; serve as a topping for chorizo burgers or with tortilla chips.

bacon, turkey and beef burgers

serves 8
prep: 15 minutes / cook: 15 minutes

A T DINNER TIME, "FAST" IS THE MUCH-NEEDED PLAN OF ACTION FOR WORKDAY meals. Increasingly, and especially during summer, cooks want the same timewise strategy to ease the kitchen crunch on weekends and holidays.

5 strips bacon, finely diced	8 hamburger rolls
1 pound each: ground beef chuck, ground turkey	8 each: slices tomato, slices onion, large lettuce leaves
1 small onion, finely chopped	½ cup cilantro leaves
¾ teaspoon chili powder	¾ cup salsa
Seasoned salt, freshly ground pepper to taste	Optional garnishes: Cheddar or Monterey jack cheese, sliced avocado
Dash hot red pepper sauce	

① Fry the bacon until crisp. Drain and transfer to a bowl. Add meats, onion and seasonings. Mix lightly, just enough to combine. Shape into 8 patties, taking care not to pack the meat too tightly.

② Prepare a medium-hot charcoal fire. Grill the burgers, 6 inches from the heat source, turning once, until they are cooked as desired, about 6 to 7 minutes per side for medium-rare. Toast rolls on the grill for the last minute or so.

③ To serve, layer the tomato slices, onion and lettuce on the rolls. Top with burgers. Sprinkle with cilantro; spoon salsa on top. Garnish with cheese and avocado if you like.

flank steak 4 ways

serves 6–8
prep: 15 minutes / marinate: 4–8 hours / cook: 10 minutes

AS GRILLING SEASON OPENS, THE SEASONED COOK WILL REACH FOR FLANK steak—it's still affordable, it takes only moments to cook, and its deeply beefy flavor can't be matched by other steaks. Try these grilling tips with four international flares to choose from. The Thai version (p. 176) includes a classic crying tiger marinade and is served with a chunky sweet-hot Thai-style relish. A Mediterranean flank steak (p. 177) has an Arabic influence, with a lemony marinade and the fiery Yemeni sauce called zhug. A Cuban twist offers a citrus-bright marinade and a variation on a churrasco sauce (p. 179). And, finally, there's an Italian-influenced flank steak with a rosemary-rich marinade and a potent lemon-rosemary sauce (p. 178). Pick your sauce and marinade, and follow the same grilling instructions.

1 flank steak, 2 to 2½ pounds   See marinade and sauce recipes that follow

① Place marinade in a dish large enough to hold the flank steak; add steak, turning to coat; cover and refrigerate, 4 to 8 hours.

② Prepare the grill with a hot fire and the grate about 2 inches above the coals.

③ Remove the flank steak from the marinade, discarding marinade. Pat steak dry with paper towels. Oil the grill grate with some vegetable oil on a paper towel. Place the flank steak on the hot grate; cook, undisturbed, 3 minutes. Turn the steak 45 degrees; cook 2 minutes longer. Flip the steak; cook, 3 minutes. Let the steak rest for 10 minutes before carving.

④ Slice the steak across the grain, angling the knife blade at a 45-degree angle. Spoon some of the sauce over each portion; pass the rest at the table.

continued

flank steak 4 ways

(continued)

TIPS

☞ The flank steak, which comes from the part of the cow's belly closest to the hind legs, is lean and muscular. It's a thin cut, rarely more than three-quarters of an inch thick in the middle, and it will come from your butcher trimmed of its cap of fat. You can expect a whole flank steak to weigh 2 to 2½ pounds, just right to serve six to eight people (or three to four, with delectable leftovers to use atop a salad the next night). The middle of the steak will be thickest, with the meat thinning at one end.

☞ Because flank is a thin cut compared with a strip or a rib-eye, for example, it needs only a brief turn on a very hot, well-preheated grill. Flank steak should always be cooked rare to medium-rare. If the heathens among your group want meat that is more well-done, give them the pieces from the thin end.

☞ Room-temperature flank steak cooks to perfection over a hot fire in just 8 minutes—4 minutes on each side—so pull your marinating flank steak out of the fridge at least an hour before cooking. Because flank steak is so lean, you definitely need to oil your hot grill grate just before laying the meat on it. To get the beautiful cross-hatching of sear marks, however, 4 minutes isn't quite enough. One surface should be the "presentation side" and give that side 3 minutes—without moving the meat, before shifting it 45 degrees on the grill for another 2 minutes. Then turn the steak and grill it for only 3 minutes on the other side. Be sure to let the steak rest for about 10 minutes before carving.

☞ Flank steak has a definite grain; the fibers of the muscle run from end to end, not from side to side. If you don't heed this grain in carving, the steak will be tough to chew. Many sources recommend carving the steak across the grain—from side to side—into slices about one-quarter-inch thick. You'll get the best result, however, if you carve across the grain and angle the blade of your knife to about 45 degrees. The slices will look more impressive, to be sure, but, more important, they'll also be more tender and succulent.

crying tiger flank steak marinade
with sweet-hot thai relish

prep: 15 minutes

MARINATE THE STEAK FOR 4 TO 8 HOURS, NO LONGER. MARINADES WITH citrus juice can toughen meat if left to marinate too long. Remember to remove the steak from the refrigerator at least an hour before cooking.

MARINADE:

¼ cup fish sauce

2 tablespoons soy sauce

1 tablespoon sugar

3 cloves garlic, minced

Juice of 1 lime

SAUCE:

5 small, fresh red hot chilies, such as chile de arbol, pequin or bird

2 Roma tomatoes

1 small onion, coarsely chopped

1 red bell pepper, coarsely chopped

4 large cloves garlic, coarsely chopped

¼ cup each: fish sauce, sugar, fresh lime juice (about 2 limes)

① For the marinade, combine fish sauce, soy sauce, sugar and 3 cloves garlic in a blender or food processor. Blend until mixture is well combined.

② For the sauce, toast the chilies in a dry heavy skillet over medium heat; remove when the chilies are fragrant. Add the tomatoes to the skillet; sear them on all sides, letting the skin char slightly. When the chilies have cooled, seed them if desired. Place chilies, tomatoes, onion, bell pepper, garlic, fish sauce, sugar and lime juice in a blender or food processor; whiz until they form a chunky puree. Place sauce into a small bowl; set aside for serving.

flank steak levantine marinade
with yemeni hot sauce

prep: 30 minutes

AYOGURT MARINADE HELPS FLAVORS PENETRATE AND TENDERIZES MEAT slightly. This one would also be good for beef or lamb kebabs. Remember to remove the steak from the refrigerator at least one hour before cooking. If you have leftover zhug, place it in a small jar and cover it with olive oil; it will keep, refrigerated, for about 1 month.

MARINADE:

1 cup plain full-fat yogurt

¼ cup olive oil

2 tablespoons tomato paste

1 tablespoon coarse salt

2 teaspoons each: ground cumin, garlic powder, smoked paprika

½ teaspoon each: cinnamon, ground ginger, ground cardamom

SAUCE:

1 pound hot green chilies, such as serrano or jalapeno

5 whole heads of garlic, peeled

1 bunch cilantro, coarsely chopped (stems and all)

1 bunch flat-leaf parsley, coarsely chopped (stems and all)

1 teaspoon ground cumin

Juice of 1 lemon, optional

Salt

① For the marinade, combine the yogurt, olive oil, tomato paste, salt, cumin, garlic powder, smoked paprika, cinnamon, ground ginger and ground cardamom in a blender or food processor. Whiz until well blended.

② For the sauce, seed the chilies, if you prefer. Combine chilies, garlic, cilantro, parsley and cumin in a food processor or blender; whiz until a thick paste forms. If the mixture is too thick, add lemon juice to thin to desired consistency. Add salt to taste.

tuscan flank steak marinade
with lemon-rosemary sauce

serves 6–8

prep: 25 minutes / marinate: 4–8 hours / cook: 10 minutes

SAVE A FEW SPRIGS OF ROSEMARY TO USE AS BASTING BRUSHES TO BRUSH ON A little dressing during the flank steak's last few minutes of cooking. When you're done, toss the sprigs onto the coals to create a bit of rosemary-scented smoke to flavor the meat even more.

MARINADE:

6 garlic cloves

½ cup fresh rosemary leaves

⅓ cup each: lemon juice, olive oil

1 teaspoon red pepper flakes

1 teaspoon salt

SAUCE:

Zest of 1 lemon

¼ cup freshly squeezed lemon juice

½ cup olive oil

2 teaspoons minced fresh rosemary leaves

½ teaspoon red pepper flakes

Pinch of salt

① For the marinade, combine garlic, rosemary leaves, lemon juice, olive oil, red pepper flakes and salt in a food processor or blender. Whiz until well combined. Place marinade in a dish large enough to hold the flank steak; add steak, turning to coat; cover and refrigerate 4–8 hours.

② For the sauce, combine lemon zest, lemon juice, olive oil, rosemary leaves, red pepper flakes and salt in a medium bowl; whisk to blend.

cuban flank steak
with mojo marinade and churrasco

serves 6–8
prep: 30 minutes / marinate: 4–8 hours / cook: 10 minutes

THIS MOJO MARINADE IS ALSO EXCELLENT WITH PORK OR CHICKEN. USING freshly squeezed citrus juices really makes a difference in this recipe. The churrasco is bright with citrus and fragrant with garlic and onion. Remember to remove the flank steak from the refrigerator at least one hour before cooking.

MARINADE:

6 cloves garlic, peeled

1 medium onion, coarsely chopped

1 cup freshly squeezed orange juice

½ cup freshly squeezed lime juice (about 4 limes)

¼ cup each: cilantro, flat-leaf parsley

1 teaspoon each: ground cumin, dried oregano, coarse salt, red pepper flakes

½ teaspoon black pepper

SAUCE:

5 cloves garlic

1 medium onion, coarsely chopped

½ cup freshly squeezed lemon juice

¼ cup freshly squeezed lime juice (about 2 limes)

2 teaspoons oregano

1 cup olive oil

① For the marinade, combine garlic, onion, orange juice, lime juice, cilantro, parsley, cumin, oregano, salt, red pepper flakes and black pepper in a food processor or blender; whiz until well blended. Place marinade in a dish large enough to hold the flank steak; add steak, turning to coat; cover and refrigerate 4–8 hours.

② For the sauce, combine garlic, onion, lemon juice, lime juice, oregano and olive oil in a food processor or blender; whiz until well combined.

butterflied leg of lamb

serves 10

prep: 10 minutes / marinate: Overnight / cook: 16 minutes

GRILLING A LEG OF LAMB CAN BE A LENGTHY CHORE; COOKING TIMES CAN reach two hours, and you can't wander off too far in case you need to turn the lamb or extinguish flare-ups. Once the meat is cooked, you have to figure out how to carve the lamb. Switch to a boneless, butterflied leg of lamb. The meat will look ungainly shorn of its bone. But the flavor will be all-lamb, and a butterflied piece of meat drinks in the flavors of any marinade you choose. This recipe has an Indian accent, thanks to the meat marinating overnight in spiced yogurt. You'll need to plan ahead, but it takes only a few minutes to mix the marinade. Serve the lamb with basmati rice, stir-fried spinach with charred garlic, chutney and raita, a cucumber, yogurt and mint dip.

2 cups plain Greek-style yogurt

2 tablespoons each: cumin, Madras-style curry powder

1 tablespoon Dijon mustard

1 teaspoon each: hot sauce, salt, black pepper

Juice of 1 lemon

1 leg of lamb, boned, butterflied, about 4 pounds

① Mix all the ingredients except lamb in a medium bowl. Slather the mixture over the lamb in a shallow pan; massage the meat gently to work the marinade into the tissue. Cover with plastic wrap; refrigerate overnight.

② Prepare a grill for direct, medium-high heat. Grill lamb 8 minutes per side. Check for doneness; grill until desired temperature is reached, about 15 minutes for medium. Let the lamb rest 5 minutes on cutting board. Cut the lamb into thin slices.

▮ TIPS ▮

☛ Greek-style yogurt is thicker than the ordinary stuff and holds on to the meat better during marination.

☛ Ask your butcher to bone and butterfly the lamb.

☛ Use any seasoning you like on the meat. A mix of olive oil, garlic, mustard and fresh oregano is one strategy; a spice rub accented by chipotle in adobo sauce is another.

slow lemon brisket

serves 10

prep: 10 minutes / cook: 10–12 hours

Here's a bit of culinary irony: Slow cookers make fast work of putting together a meal. Combine a few ingredients; plug in the slow cooker and, hours later, you're rewarded with complex aromas and a hearty family meal. This brisket recipe, designed for a slow cooker, was sent in by Nancy Hablutzel of Chicago. She describes this brisket as not quite traditional, but delicious with lemony overtones: "My daughter, Margo Lynn, developed it from a medieval lamb recipe for me to serve for our play-reading group when we were reading a Shakespearean play from that period. It was a big hit." Best of all—the slow cooker allows you to have a piping hot meal without heating up the kitchen.

2 ribs celery, halved lengthwise

2 onions, quartered

1 first-cut or flat-cut (leaner section) beef brisket, about 4 pounds, trimmed

2 lemons, cut into thin slices

1 cup raisins or to taste

1 teaspoon salt

Freshly ground pepper

2 low-sodium beef bouillon cubes, dissolved in 2 cups water

① Line the bottom of a large slow cooker with the celery and onions; top with brisket. Place lemon slices and raisins on the brisket; season with salt and pepper to taste. Add dissolved bouillon.

② Cook on low until meat is fork-tender, about 10–12 hours. Remove meat to cutting board; let stand 15 minutes. Skim fat from cooking broth. Adjust seasonings, if needed. Remove lemon slices; cut in half. Pour broth into a serving bowl; add lemons. Slice meat across the grain into thin slices; serve with the broth and lemons.

low country boil

serves 4

prep: 40 minutes / cook: 1 hour, 15 minutes

MARK STEUER IS A SOUTH CAROLINA-BRED CHEF WHO, AT HIS WICKER PARK restaurant Carriage House, has brought the rustic charm of a low country boil to the Midwest. It's a splendidly earthy tradition, which comes from the southeastern corner of the U.S. and is sometimes called Frogmore Stew (named for a place, not an ingredient). Simply, it's a one-pot masterpiece of shellfish, red potatoes, corn-on-the cob and a little chaurice sausage (Carolina's answer to Andouille), all spilled across a newspaper-covered picnic table with effortless elan. Hang a rope of string lights above the table, and you're Instagram-ready. Steuer says growing up in Charleston, the low country boil was the traditional feast at family get-togethers. "It's kind of interactive," he says. "Everyone gathers around the table together and gets their hands dirty."

But dirty in a good way. "Some people think it's not pretty," the chef admits. "But the simplicity and quality of the ingredients is what makes it beautiful."

24 head-on large shrimp

1½ pounds chaurice sausage (see note), cut into 1½-inch segments

24 clams

1 pound red potatoes, quartered and cooked

4 ears corn, quartered

1 Vidalia onion, julienned

1 head fennel, shaved

2 tablespoons Old Bay butter (recipe follows)

4 quarts shrimp and corn stock (recipe follows)

4 lemons, halved and grilled

① In a large pot, sear the shrimp and sausage until slightly colored on the outside. Add the clams, potatoes, corn, onion, fennel, Old Bay butter and stock; cover. Steam until the clams open.

② Place the lemons on top. Serve.

NOTE: If you cannot find chaurice, substitute andouille.

old bay butter

serves 4
prep: 5 minutes

2 tablespoons softened butter

2 teaspoons Old Bay Seasoning

① In a bowl, whisk together the butter and Old Bay Seasoning until smooth and fully combined.

shrimp and corn stock

serves 4
prep: 30 minutes / cook: 1 hour, 20 minutes

5 pounds fish bones

4 ounces shrimp shells

4 whole corn cobs, corn removed

1 Vidalia onion, chopped

3 ribs celery, chopped

1 fennel bulb, chopped

1 tablespoon fennel seed

6 quarts ice water

① Combine the fish bones, shrimp shells, corn cobs, onion, celery, fennel, fennel seed and ice water in a large pot; bring to a simmer. Reduce heat to low and let simmer, 1 hour. Remove impurities that collect on the surface with a ladle. Strain through a cheesecloth.

michigan baked beans

serves 4–6

prep: 10 minutes / soak: overnight / cook: 3 hours

WELL, YES, YOU COULD JUST OPEN A CAN. BUT HOMEMADE BAKED BEANS OFFER much more than even the best Jay Bush can trot out. They offer a connection to the past. Della Lutes opens her 1935 classic "The Country Kitchen" with an accounting of her father's birthday feast in 1882: "A great pan of beans was baked, nice, white Michigan (or New York State) beans, soaked overnight, parboiled in the early morning with a pinch of soda, then washed in cold water and boiled again with a slab of salt pork and an onion, until the outer skin burst. They were then drained and seasoned with salt, pepper, mustard, a little vinegar and brown sugar, turned into a heavy tin pan, with the pork, slashed across the rind into small squares, adorning the centre, and baked until the beans were brought to a mealy consistency suitable for slicing when cold." That's the way they made baked beans in Jackson County, Mich., more than a century ago. Here's the way former Tribune reporter and Jackson County native Robin Mather Jenkins makes them in her kitchen today.

1 **pound dried navy beans, rinsed**

½ **pound salt pork, in one piece**

1 **large onion, stuck with two cloves**

¼ **teaspoon baking soda**

2 **tablespoons coarse brown mustard, such as Zatarain's Creole**

¼ **cup cider vinegar**

½ **cup packed brown sugar**

½ **teaspoon salt**

　Freshly ground pepper

① Place the beans in a large saucepan. Cover with cold water by a depth of 2 inches; soak at room temperature overnight. Drain; rinse. Drain; return the beans to the pan. Cover with cold water to a depth of 2 inches.

② Add the salt pork, onion and baking soda to the beans. Cook over medium heat until the skins on the beans burst when you blow gently on one, about 1 hour. Drain the beans. Discard the onion; reserve the salt pork. (Reserve the broth if you like as a soup base.)

③ Heat the oven to 300 degrees. Place the beans in a large heavy casserole with a close-fitting lid. Combine mustard, vinegar and brown sugar; blend into beans. Season with salt and pepper to taste. Cross-hatch the rind of the salt pork by making ¼-inch deep slashes in two directions. Nestle the salt pork in the casserole. Cover; cook, stirring occasionally, until the beans are very tender, 2–3 hours.

green chili with chicken

serves 6

prep: 30 minutes / cook: 1 hour, 26 minutes

ASK A TEXAN, AND HE'LL TELL YOU: CHILI DOESN'T HAVE BEANS. As it happens, we agree with that.

Ask a New Mexican, and he'll tell you that chili doesn't even have to have beef. We agree with that too. As often as not, we make chicken chili, rather than the traditional "bowl of red" that frontiersman Kit Carson famously pined for. This easy, relatively lean chili is rich and satisfying, but it won't be super spicy; slip in some jalapenos if you want more heat, or offer chopped chilies at the table so diners can customize their servings. The mild fresh New Mexico chilies we use in this dish are sometimes labeled Anaheim; they're 6 to 8 inches long and deep green. Use poblanos instead if they're easier for you to find, but be aware that poblanos can pack a bit of a punch. Best to taste them to find out. It's worth taking the time to roast your own chilies. Their flavor will be bright and their texture toothsome.

8 New Mexico or poblano chilies	3 cans (14 ounces each) chicken broth
2 jalapeno chilies, optional	1 can (14½ ounces) diced tomatoes
¼ cup olive oil	1 teaspoon dried oregano
2 onions, chopped	¼ cup whipping cream or half-and-half
2 cloves garlic, minced	2 tablespoons cornmeal
1 teaspoon ground cumin	Chopped chilies, crumbled Mexican cheese, chopped onion, minced cilantro, salsa
1½ pounds boneless skinless chicken breasts	

① Heat the broiler or a heavy skillet over medium heat; roast the chilies, turning, until blackened on all sides, about 8 minutes. Transfer to a plastic or paper bag; set aside to cool. Peel away blackened skins. (It's OK if some charred bits remain.) Seed chilies; chop. Set aside.

② Heat the oil in a Dutch oven over medium heat. Stir in onions, garlic and cumin; cook, stirring occasionally, until onions are translucent and tender, about 10 minutes. Meanwhile, cut the chicken into ½-inch square pieces; transfer to the Dutch oven. Cook, stirring once or twice, until chicken is opaque, about 8 minutes.

③ Add chicken broth, tomatoes, oregano and reserved chilies. Increase heat to high; heat to a boil. Cover; reduce heat to a simmer. Cook, stirring occasionally, about 50 minutes. Stir in cream and cornmeal; cook 10 minutes. Pass the garnishes at the table.

cool treats

DESSERTS

butterscotch praline ice cream sundae p. 193
« hawaiian icy p. 195
unbelievable peanut cookies p. 196
poached peaches with raspberries p. 197
peach crisp p. 198
dessert bruschetta p. 201
strawberry muffins p. 203
blueberry delight p. 204

butterscotch praline ice cream sundae

makes 6 sundaes
prep: 15 minutes / cook: 12 minutes

For ice cream makers, vanilla is the badge of honor. "Vanilla is the measure of what a good ice cream tastes like, because it's the purest," says Bob Renaut, former president of Oberweis Dairy, based in North Aurora, which sells 800 percent more vanilla than second-place chocolate. "You don't have a bunch of other ingredients thrown in." This deliciously decadent recipe comes from Heather Terhune, former executive chef at Atwood Cafe.

BUTTERSCOTCH SAUCE:

1 stick (½ cup) unsalted butter
1¼ cups packed brown sugar
¾ cup each: light corn syrup, whipping cream
2 teaspoons vanilla extract
1¼ teaspoons salt

CANDIED PECANS:

12 ounces whole pecans
4 tablespoons granulated sugar
4 tablespoons butter, melted
1 teaspoon salt
1 quart premium vanilla ice cream
Whipped cream, optional

① Heat oven to 350 degrees. For sauce, put butter, brown sugar, corn syrup, cream, vanilla and salt into a heavy-duty saucepan on medium-high heat. Cook, whisking constantly, until it boils. Boil 2 minutes. Cool to room temperature, whisking occasionally so butter does not separate from mixture. (Sauce may be made ahead and refrigerated for up to 1 week.)

② For pecans, put nuts, granulated sugar, butter and salt into a stainless-steel bowl; toss until thoroughly coated. Place on cookie sheet; bake until golden brown, about 10 minutes. Do not overbake. Cool.

③ Scoop ice cream into 6 bowls. Top with about ⅓ cup of the butterscotch sauce, a few candied pecans and whipped cream.

continued

butterscotch praline ice cream sundae

(continued)

TIPS

from the International Dairy Foods Association and Oberweis Dairy to keep ice cream at peak flavor

AT THE STORE

☛ Make the ice cream aisle your last stop at the supermarket.

☛ The temperature of the freezer case should not be above minus 20 degrees. If kept at a proper temperature, ice cream will be thoroughly frozen and will feel hard.

☛ In open-top freezer cases, buy ice cream and frozen treats that are stored below the freezer line.

☛ Insulate ice cream for the ride home. When your groceries are packed, request an additional brown paper bag to insulate it.

AT HOME

☛ Don't let ice cream repeatedly soften and refreeze. When ice cream's small ice crystals melt and refreeze, they will eventually turn into large, unappetizing lumps.

☛ The freezer should be set at minus 5 to 0 degrees. Ice cream is easy to dip at 6 to 10 degrees, the ideal serving range.

☛ Store ice cream in the main part of the freezer. Do not store it in the freezer door, where it is subjected to fluctuating temperatures when the door is open and shut.

☛ Keep the ice cream container tightly closed when storing in the freezer.

☛ Don't store ice cream alongside uncovered foods; odors may penetrate ice cream and affect its flavor.

☛ For optimal storage, put the carton in a sealed freezer-safe bag.

hawaiian icy

serves 4

prep: 15 minutes / cook: 45 minutes / stand: 2 hours
pictured on p. 190

THE AIM OF THIS, LIKE ALL ICY TREATS, IS TO RENDER THE UPPER PALATE, TEETH, skull and BRAIN so frigid that for a few frozen seconds, summer itself is out cold.

1 ripe pineapple, peeled, cored, chopped

½ cup dark brown sugar

2 cups mango nectar, see note

¼ cup granulated sugar

4 cups ice cubes

Sweetened flaked coconut, optional

Gummy worms, optional

① Set pineapple chunks on a rimmed baking sheet. Sprinkle with brown sugar. Slide into a 350-degree oven and roast golden, turning once, 40 minutes. Cool. Freeze firm, 2 hours. (Slide into a ziptop bag, if working ahead.)

② Stir together mango nectar and granulated sugar in a large saucepan. Heat to a boil; lower ever so slightly and cook until syrupy, 5 minutes. Cool. Transfer to a squeeze bottle. Chill.

③ Measure 2 cups ice cubes and 1 cup pineapple chunks into the blender. Using the "snow" function, flake to bits. (Or use the "crush" function for a chunkier approach.) Scoop into two small cups. Add a squeeze of mango syrup. Dust with coconut, if you like. Add gummy worms, if you must. (Repeat with remaining ingredients.) Enjoy with sunshine.

NOTE: For mango nectar, try the juice aisle or the Mexican foods section.

unbelievable peanut cookies

makes 30 cookies
prep: 15 minutes / cook: 8–10 minutes

THIS COOKIE RECIPE WAS SENT IN BY MARY ANN PUCHALSKI OF ELMHURST, who says they are great for picnics. Made without flour, this dough bakes into soft, candylike cookies in about 8 minutes. We also liked the more traditional peanut butter cookie texture produced by baking them 2 minutes longer.

1 cup each: peanut butter, sugar

1 egg

½ teaspoon vanilla

30 solid chocolate stars, or other small chocolate candy pieces

① Heat oven to 350 degrees. Mix peanut butter, sugar, egg and vanilla in medium bowl. Form dough into teaspoon-sized balls; place on a cookie sheet. Press a chocolate star into the center of each cookie.

② Bake 8 minutes for soft cookies, or 10 minutes for sturdier cookies. Let cookies stand 2 minutes on cookie sheet. Transfer to a cooling rack; cool.

poached peaches with raspberries

serves 8

prep: 10 minutes / cook: 10 minutes / chill: 30 minutes or longer

W HAT'S MORE DELICIOUS THAN FRESH PEACHES? FRESH PEACHES POACHED in wine, lightly scented with rosemary, honey and fresh raspberries.

3 cups Sauternes or late-harvest riesling	2 tablespoons honey
1½ cups water	2 large branches fresh rosemary
½ cup sugar	8 large ripe peaches
	1 pint fresh raspberries

① Combine the wine, water, sugar, honey and rosemary in a large saucepan and heat to a boil. Add the peaches and cook until they are tender but not soft, 5 to 10 minutes, depending on how ripe they are. Remove from the liquid, remove the skin and return the peaches to the liquid. Cool. The peaches can be cooked up to 3 days in advance and refrigerated.

② At serving time, cut the peaches in half and remove the pits. Slice peaches. To serve as a compote, spoon about ¼ cup of the poaching liquid into 8 dessert dishes and add some peaches and raspberries. Or, serve the fruit over pound or angel food cake or ice cream. Drizzle with a small amount of the poaching liquid.

peach crisp

serves 8

prep: 30 minutes / cook: 40 minutes

THE PEACH SPORTS TWO LOOKS: FREESTONE AND CLINGSTONE. CLEAVE THE freestone to reveal a single seed, as woody, hard and bitter as its cousin, the almond. Pry it out and marvel at the poisonous heart of the seemingly sunny peach. Halve the clingstone peach at your peril. When peach season arrives, we approach the clingstone whole, saving the freestone for kitchen duty. The easygoing peach takes readily to orderly prep: blanching and skinning, slicing and sugaring, topping and baking. Hot from the oven, the baked peach wafts the scent of welcome.

TOPPING:

¾ cup slivered almonds

¾ cup flour

¼ cup granulated sugar

¼ cup light brown sugar

¼ teaspoon salt

½ cup unsalted butter, in chunks

FILLING:

3 pounds (about 8) ripe, fragrant freestone peaches

¼ cup sugar

1 tablespoon flour

½ teaspoon almond extract

① Spread nuts on a baking sheet and slide into a 350-degree oven until golden, 5 minutes. Let cool.

② For topping, measure flour, both sugars and salt into the food processor. Pulse to combine. Add nuts. Pulse a few times to break up, not pulverize, nuts. Tumble in butter; pulse to crumbly. Chill.

③ For filling, bring a large pot of water to a boil. Set a bowl of ice water nearby. Lower in peaches; let simmer until skins loosen, 10 seconds. Lift out peaches and lower into ice water. Slip off and discard skins.

④ Working over a large mixing bowl (to catch juice), slice peaches into ½-inch thick crescents.

⑤ Sprinkle peaches with sugar and flour; mix gently. Add extract; mix gently.

⑥ Scrape peach mixture into a 9-inch pie plate. Sprinkle on topping. Bake at 375 degrees, uncovered, until topping browns, fruit bubbles and the whole thing smells nutty and delightful, 40 minutes. Cool on a rack. Serve warm.

dessert bruschetta

serves 12
prep: 8 minutes / cook: 1 minute

Most people think of bruschetta as a summertime appetizer. The Italians love to use up fresh tomatoes mixed with just a hint of basil and fresh garlic, and for parties, it's always a hit. This sweet-and-salty bruschetta makes a unique, passed dessert that will be popular in any setting, mainly because it uses high-quality ingredients in small proportions and everything can be bought in containers, then assembled at the last minute as you're making coffee. The only caveat is that this dish will require a trip to one or more specialty markets. Fresh ricotta can be found in the cheese section of several specialty stores and Italian markets; dulce de leche can be purchased at Williams-Sonoma or on Amazon.com. High-quality sea salt is more readily available in specialty stores. The hazelnut-chocolate spread (Nutella) is available in many supermarkets and specialty stores. Call stores ahead of time to make sure they have the products in stock. Alternatives to the bread might include purchased biscotti cookies or poundcake squares.

1 baguette or narrow French bread loaf, sliced ¼-inch thick

½ cup each: hazelnut-chocolate spread, fresh ricotta

¼ cup dulce de leche

1 tablespoon fleur de sel or other sea salt

① Heat broiler; place bread slices on baking sheet. Broil until lightly browned, about 1 minute.

② Spread 2 teaspoons of the hazelnut spread onto each slice; top each with a small dollop of ricotta cheese. Drizzle a small amount of dulce de leche on top of the cheese. Top each with a pinch of sea salt.

strawberry muffins

makes 12 muffins

prep: 15 minutes / cook: 25 minutes

STRAWBERRIES ARE THE SYMBOL OF VENUS, THE GODDESS OF LOVE; THEIR heart-shaped appearance alone inspires a certain passion, but it's the flavor that seals the deal. These fragrant muffins were developed in the Tribune test kitchen.

2 cups flour	2 eggs
2 teaspoons baking powder	1 stick (½ cup) unsalted butter, melted
½ teaspoon salt	½ cup whole milk
1 cup sugar, plus 6 teaspoons	1 teaspoon vanilla extract
1½ cups chopped strawberries	

(1) Heat oven to 375 degrees. Combine flour, baking powder, salt and 1 cup of the sugar in medium bowl. Toss in strawberries; set aside. Beat together eggs, butter, milk and vanilla in small bowl. Add wet ingredients to dry ingredients; stir until just combined.

(2) Spoon batter into muffin tins lined with paper liners. Sprinkle ½ teaspoon of sugar on top of each muffin. Bake until toothpick inserted into center comes out clean, about 25 minutes.

blueberry delight

serves 6
prep: 20 minutes

THIS IS AN ENTIRELY RAW DESSERT, ADAPTED FROM A RECIPE POPULAR AT Karyn Calabrese's Chicago restaurants focused on raw food. In this recipe, fresh blueberries are topped with a healthful crumble mixture. Look for ingredients in health food stores.

1 teaspoon each: almond meal, flax seed
½ teaspoon wheat germ
2 cups raw organic cashews

1 cup spring water
½ cup organic maple syrup
1 tablespoon vanilla extract
1½ pints blueberries

① Combine almond meal, flax seed and wheat germ in a small bowl; set aside.

② Process cashews and water in a blender until almost smooth. Add maple syrup and vanilla; process until smooth.

③ Divide blueberries among 6 bowls; sprinkle equally with almond meal mixture. Top with cashew sauce to taste.

credits

article and recipe credits

Basic backyard lemonade, page 10.
"A summer squeeze of ease: Quest for ideal quencher leads right back home, to lemonade." By William Rice, August 14, 2002.

Fruit smoothie, page 13.
"A cup to go: Athletes' thirst for smoothies has benefits and pitfalls." By Bob Condor, March 22, 2000.

Lemon balm iced tea, page 15.
"Drinking in the garden: Fresh herbs can push beverages into bold, sparkling directions." By Renee Enna; recipe by David Burns of the former Le Meridien Chicago, August 25, 2004.

Herb-flavored simple syrups, page 15.
"Drinking in the garden: Fresh herbs can push beverages into bold, sparkling directions." By Renee Enna; recipe by David Burns of the former Le Meridien Chicago, August 25, 2004.

Caipirinha, page 16; Simple syrup, page 17.
"Latin cool: Sizzling citrus cocktails make a splash in Chicago." By Judy Hevrdejs; recipe by adapted from a recipe by Nacional 27 restaurant, August 11, 1999.

Mojito, page 18.
"Extreme leisure: 20 ways to indulge in the simple joys of summer; fantasy island; the best vacation is just a daydream, and a cold drink, away." By Leah Eskin, June 5, 2005.

Batida, page 19.
"Latin cool: Sizzling citrus cocktails make a splash in Chicago." By Judy Hevrdejs, August 11, 1999 .

The Mambo, page 20.
"Latin cool: Sizzling citrus cocktails make a splash in Chicago." By Judy Hevrdejs; recipe adapted from a recipe by Mambo Grill, August 11, 1999.

Pisco sour, page 21.
"Latin cool: Sizzling citrus cocktails make a splash in Chicago." By Judy Hevrdejs; recipe adapted from a recipe by Rinconcito Sudamericano, August 11, 1999.

Chocolate-covered grasshopper, page 22.
"The plain truth: Vanilla remains the No. 1 flavor of ice cream sold in the U.S. Now it's getting richer." By Renee Enna, July 10, 2002.

Raspberry-lemon slam, page 24.
"A summer squeeze of ease: Quest for ideal quencher leads right back home, to lemonade." By William Rice, August 14, 2002.

Daiquiri, page 25.
"Extreme leisure: 20 ways to indulge in the simple joys of summer; fantasy island; the best vacation is just a daydream, and a cold drink, away." By Leah Eskin, June 5, 2005.

Homemade limoncello, page 26.
"Sips of sunshine: Limoncello's bright flavor reflects Amalfi's sun-drenched coast." By Joe Gray; recipe adapted from a recipe by Tom Beckman, an instructor at the Cooking and Hospitality Institute of Chicago, October 8, 2003 .

Sorrento sunset, page 28.
"Sips of sunshine: Limoncello's bright flavor reflects Amalfi's sun-drenched coast." By Joe Gray; recipe adapted from a recipe served at The Italian Village Restaurants, October 8, 2003.

Nevisian smile, page 29.
"Going tropical: Chicago's summer heat inspires cocktails with exotic twists." By Tom Connors, July 23, 2003.

Le Jardin des Huguenots, page 32.
"Now with more punch! Surprising flavors spike the popularity of the centuries-old sip." By Judy Hevrdejs; recipe by Roderick Hale Weaver at Husk restaurant in Charleston, S.C, December 29, 2013.

Red sangria, page 31.
"Mixing it up with wine: Sangrias and spritzers bring a refreshing edge to summertime sipping." By Bill Daley; recipe by Fabian Padilla of Chicago, August 23, 2006.

Mango, plum and peach sangria, page 33.
"Mixing it up with wine: Sangrias and spritzers bring a refreshing edge to summertime sipping." By Bill Daley; recipe by Fabian Padilla of Chicago, August 23, 2006.

Amere, page 35.
"The flavor is fall: Four Chicago pros share the ingredients that spark their fall parties and evoke the richest season." By Chris Lamorte, Oct. 13, 2013.

Bella Fragola, page 36.
"Drinking in the garden," By Lauren Viera, May 8, 2011.

House G+T, page 40; Tonic syrup, page 41.
"Cooler quencher." By Bill Daley, June 1 2014.

Smoked salmon mousse, page 44.
"Party tonight! Is it that time of year already? Yes, and these make-ahead nibbles can feed the crowd and calm the host." By Kristin Eddy, William Rice, Carol Mighton Haddix, Renee Enna, Andy Badeker, Donna Pierce and Steve Dolinsky; recipe by William Rice. November 13, 2002.

Snappy sausage and cucumber rounds with mustard, page 47.
"Party tonight! Is it that time of year already? Yes, and these make-ahead nibbles can feed the crowd and calm the host." By Kristin Eddy, William Rice, Carol Mighton Haddix, Renee Enna, Andy Badeker, Donna Pierce and Steve Dolinsky; recipe by Carol Mighton Haddix, November 13, 2002 .

Wonton chicken bites, page 48.
"Party tonight! Is it that time of year already? Yes, and these make-ahead nibbles can feed the crowd and calm the host." By Kristin Eddy, William Rice, Carol Mighton Haddix, Renee Enna, Andy Badeker, Donna Pierce and Steve Dolinsky; recipe by Donna Pierce, November 13, 2002.

Simple ceviche, page 51.
"Chop, mix, done: Ceviche delivers fresh, tangy flavors in no time." By James P. DeWan, May 5, 2010.

Nut stuffing for vegetables, page 52.
"Taking the raw route: A new food movement gains attention with its no-cooking, fresh-from-the-garden, approach to diet." By William Rice; recipe adapted from a recipe from Karyn Calabrese, July 30, 2003.

Shrimp on pesto rounds, page 53.
"Tiny bites: Finger foods from around the world are the antidote to ho-hum entertaining." By Nancy Ross Ryan, May 1, 1996.

Olive-avocado dim sum, page 54.
"Taking the raw route: A new food movement gains attention with its no-cooking, fresh-from-the-garden, approach to diet." By William Rice; recipe adapted from a recipe from Karyn Calabrese, July 30, 2003.

Asian summer rolls, page 57.
"Wrapping up the holiday: Ethnic sandwiches pack up and go with a minimum of fuss for a relaxing Labor Day picnic." By Robin Mather Jenkins, September 1, 2004.

Creamy basil-onion dip, page 58.
"Dip right in: Global flavors and fresh ideas bring a classic party food into the 21st Century." By Emily Nunn; recipe by Renee Enna, June 18, 2008.

Vegetable-stuffed deviled eggs, page 60.
"Beat the heat: 12 refreshing dishes take the hot-stove duty out of those blistering August days." By Andrew Schloss, August 1, 1991.

Cheese and rye cocktail sandwiches, page 61.
"Party tonight! Is it that time of year already? Yes, and these make-ahead nibbles can feed the crowd and calm the host." By Kristin Eddy, William Rice, Carol Mighton Haddix, Renee Enna, Andy Badeker, Donna Pierce and Steve Dolinsky; recipe by Kristin Eddy, November 13, 2002.

Mexican pinwheels, page 62.
"The food guide." Recipe by Lois Starkey of Norridge, August 1, 1991.

Chilled white gazpacho, page 63.
"Cool it: Throw a summer party without ever breaking a sweat." By Bill Daley; recipe by Lee Wolen of Boka restaurant, July 6, 2014.

Pecorino crisp, page 64.
"The foodie fix: What you've got: A season's worth of food-obsessed party guests; What you need: Three chef-designed hits that will knock them into Instagram nirvana." By Bill Daley; recipe by Jake Bickelhaput of 42 Grams restaurant, October 5, 2014.

Prosciutto wrapped figs, page 67.
"The flavor is fall: Four Chicago pros share the ingredients that spark their fall parties and evoke the richest season." By Chris Lamorte, October 13, 2013.

Empress coleslaw, page 70.
"Summer and slaw: Cabbage's most famous role follows a new script in time for the holiday weekend." By William Rice, August 28, 2002.

Italian slaw for a crowd, page 72.
"Summer and slaw: Cabbage's most famous role follows a new script in time for the holiday weekend." By William Rice; recipe adapted from a recipe from David Shea of Twelve 12 restaurant. August 28, 2002.

Baked potato salad, page 73.
"Reinterpreting a classic: Creative approaches put a fresh spin on the all-American potato salad." By Kristin Eddy, July 4, 2001.

Red, white and blue potato salad, page 75.
"Reinterpreting a classic: Creative approaches put a fresh spin on the all-American potato salad." By Kristin Eddy, July 4, 2001.

Fingerling potato salad with tarragon, page 76.
"Reinterpreting a classic: Creative approaches put a fresh spin on the all-American potato salad." By Kristin Eddy, July 4, 2001.

Potato salad Nicoise, page 79.
"Reinterpreting a classic: Creative approaches put a fresh spin on the all-American potato salad." By Kristin Eddy, July 4, 2001.

Curried sweet potato salad with golden raisins and toasted almonds, page 80.
"Reinterpreting a classic: Creative approaches put a fresh spin on the all-American potato salad." By Kristin Eddy, July 4, 2001.

Lentil salad with lemon dressing, page 81.
"Salad daze: Choices abound to dress up and combine greens for outdoor menus." By William Rice, July 9, 2003.

Wild rice salad with fennel and mustard dressing, page 82.
"Back to the wild: Texas wild rice, a relative of northern varieties, is a poster child for the argument to protect native species." By William Rice, recipe adapted from a recipe in "Prairie Home Cooking," by Judith M. Fertig, August 27, 2003.

Pasta salad with shallots, herbs and tomato compote, page 84.
"Bastille meal: A holiday menu that lets you celebrate with French Elan." By Pat Dailey, July 12, 1995.

Roasted pepper and onion salad with goat cheese and orange, page 85.
"Bastille meal: A holiday menu that lets you celebrate with French Elan." By Pat Dailey, July 12, 1995.

Marshall Field's lemon pasta salad, page 87.
"Fresh basil stars in pasta salad." By Donna Pierce; recipe from Marshall Field's provided by Kathy Finn of Evanston, August 13, 2008.

Roasted vegetable salad with apple vinaigrette, page 89.
"Salad daze: Choices abound to dress up and combine greens for outdoor menus." By William Rice, July 9, 2003.

Summer salad with fresh citrus vinaigrette, page 90.
"Salad daze: Choices abound to dress up and combine greens for outdoor menus." By William Rice, July 9, 2003.

Abundant sorrel salad, page 92.
"Schooled in salad." By Leah Eskin, August 10, 2014.

Asparagus salad with red onion, tomato and basil, page 94.
"Tender vegetables make fine summer salads." By Abby Mandel, June 17, 2001.

Cauliflower and red pepper salad with sweet mustard dressing, page 95.
"Tender vegetables make fine summer salads." By Abby Mandel, June 17, 2001.

Asian salad of sugar snap peas, mushrooms and cilantro leaves, page 96.
"Tender vegetables make fine summer salads." By Abby Mandel, June 17, 2001.

Swiss cheese salad, page 97.
"Salad daze: Choices abound to dress up and combine greens for outdoor menus." By William Rice, July 9, 2003.

Mixed greens with marinated flank steak and herb vinaigrette, page 98.
"Out of ideas for dinner? We get inspiration from cooks who can't be beat by the heat." By William Rice, July 18, 2001.

Quick crab and avocado salad, page 99.
"Holding on to summer: All the tastes of season in the palm of your hand." By Julia Edwards, September 15, 2010.

Hot or cold beef-soba noodle salad, page 100.
"Hot or cold, entree salad works for dinner." By Renee Enna, June 2, 2004.

Summer bean salad with Sun Gold tomatoes, herbs, smoked trout, goat cheese dressing, page 102.
"Recipes for market's bounty in cookbook." By Joe Gray; recipe by Chef Jason Hammel and originally published in "The Green City Market Cookbook," July 9, 2014.

Grilled shrimp and pineapple salad, page 105.
"Give your entree salad tropical flair." By Renee Enna, Tribune Newspapers, May 26, 2010.

Napa slaw with charred salmon, page 106.
"Summer and slaw: Cabbage's most famous role follows a new script in time for the holiday weekend." By William Rice; recipe by Michael Altenberg of Campagnola and Bistro Campagne, August 28, 2002.

Seared scallops with a fennel, olive and red onion salad, page 107.
"Cool it: Throw a summer party without ever breaking a sweat." By Bill Daley; recipe by Lee Wolen of Boka restaurant. July 6, 2014.

Papa Eloy's tuna salad, page 108.
"For papa, everything tastes better with a Mexican spin." By Michell Eloy, June 26, 2013.

New Nicoise salad, page 111.
"How to pair wine: This week: Nicoise salad." By Bill St. John; recipe by Carol Mighton Haddix, June 6, 2012.

Spinach and fingerling potato salad with warm bacon dressing, page 112.
"Back to bacon: A breakfast staple renews its image with new artisan brands." By Kristin Eddy, May 15, 2002.

Chioggia beet salad, page 115.
"Farm fresh chefs." By Judy Hevrdejs, May 9, 2010.

Beet carpaccio, page 117.
"The foodie fix: What you've got: a season's worth of food-obsessed party guests; What you need: Three chef-designed hits that will knock them into Instagram nirvana." By Bill Daley; recipe by Anthony Martin of Tru restaurant, October 5, 2014.

Shrimp sandwiches with chili mayonnaise, page 122.
"One sophisticated sandwich." By Emily Nunn, September 3, 2008.

Tuna sandwich, page 124; Quickie aioli, page 125.
"Home on the range: Tried and true." By Leah Eskin, July 31, 2011.

Grilled English Cheddar sandwich with smoked bacon and apple, page 126.
"Back to bacon: A breakfast staple renews its image with new artisan brands." By Kristin Eddy; recipe adapted from Artisianal restaurant, May 15, 2002.

Angie Johnson's pasties, page 127.
"Pass the pasties: Hand-filling savory turnovers have a history in Michigan." By Jane Ammeson; recipe by Angie Johnson, February 24, 1999.

Torta Americana, page 129.
"Wrapping up the holiday: Ethnic sandwiches pack up and go with a minimum of fuss for a relaxing Labor Day picnic." By Robin Mather Jenkins, September 1, 2004.

Tofu po' boy, page 131.
"Pack 'n' go: 3 make-ahead sandwiches for easy Labor Day outings."By Bill Daley; recipe adapted from a recipe from Mark Shadle of G-Zen restaurant in Branford, Conn., August 27, 2014.

Better than BLTs, page 132.
"Wrapping up the holiday: Ethnic sandwiches pack up and go with a minimum of fuss for a relaxing Labor Day picnic." By Robin Mather Jenkins, September 1, 2004.

Medianoche, page 134.
"Wrapping up the holiday: Ethnic sandwiches pack up and go with a minimum of fuss for a relaxing Labor Day picnic." By Robin Mather Jenkins, September 1, 2004.

Baja fish tacos, page 137; Salsa fresca, page 138; Creamy cabbage slaw, page 138.
"Baja at home: Fried or grilled, fish tacos put fresh spin on Labor Day cookouts." By Lisa Futterman, August 31, 2011.

Ethiopian chicken wraps, page 140.
"Wrapping up the holiday: Ethnic sandwiches pack up and go with a minimum of fuss for a relaxing Labor Day picnic." By Robin Mather Jenkins; recipe adapted from a recipe in Dironda Hafner's "A Taste of Africa," September 1, 2004.

Mackerel, carrot & herb salad sandwiches, page 143.
"Cooks come home." By Cindy Dampier, February 10, 2013.

Chicken salad sandwich, page 144; Herb aioli, page 144.
"Better bite." By William Hageman, February 12, 2012.

Grilled tomato and olive pizza, page 148.
"Dinner tonight: Quick entrees for weekday dining: Pizza takes to the grill." By Donna Pierce, August 13, 2008.

Grilled eggplant, page 150; Crispy noodle pillow, page 151.
"Home on the range: Bumper crop: Plants are flaunting their fertility." by Leah Eskin, August 1, 2004.

Grilled veggies, page 152.
"How to pair wine: This week: Grilled veggies." By Bill St. John; recipe adapted from a recipe by Donna Pierce, July 10, 2013.

Fish tacos locos, page 153.
"Baja at home: Fried or grilled, fish tacos put fresh spin on Labor Day cookouts." By Lisa Futterman, August 31, 2011.

Jerk chicken pinchos, page 154; Salsa verde, page 155.
"Home on the range: Street eats, anytime." By Leah Eskin, June 19, 2011.

BBQ chicken, page 156; Apricot barbecue sauce, page 157.
"Home on the range: Back at the backyard barbecue." By Leah Eskin, May 20, 2012.

Simple summer chicken, page 159.
Roaming free: Two farmers, a few friends and the freshest organic meat from these parts." By Leah Eskin, June 13, 2004.

Caribbean-style garlic-soaked shrimp, page 160.
"Latin-ize your grill: Draw on traditional cuisines to punch up the flavor for summer menus." By Lisa Futterman, May 30, 2012.

Grilled branzino with smoked salt and pepper, page 163.
"The summer pantry." By David Syrek, May 9, 2010.

Grilled octopus salad with grapefruit balsamic vinegar, page 164.
"Art of the condiment." By Josh Noel, March 11, 2012.

Grilled shrimp with sambal, page 167.
"Sizzling sambal." By Bill Daley, June 12, 2011.

Carne asada with chimichurri, page 169.
"Latin-ize your grill: Draw on traditional cuisines to punch up the flavor for summer menus." By Lisa Futterman, May 30, 2012.

Chorizo burgers with queso fresco, page 171; Avocado salsa, page 171.
"Latin-ize your grill: Draw on traditional cuisines to punch up the flavor for summer menus." By Lisa Futterman, May 30, 2012.

Bacon, turkey and beef burgers, page 172.
"Cook's holiday: Celebrate the Fourth with an easy outdoor menu." By Pat Dailey, June 28, 1995.

Flank steak 4 ways, page 173; Crying tiger flank steak marinade with sweet-hot Thai relish, page 176; Flank steak Levantine marinade with Yemeni hot sauce, page 177; Tuscan flank steak marinade with lemon-rosemary sauce, page 178; Cuban flank steak with mojo marinade and churrasco, page 179.
"The right cut: Tricks to getting the best out of the griller's friend: Flank steak." By Robin Mather, May 28, 2014.

Butterflied leg of lamb, page 181.
"Fast food: 30-minute entrees for time-pressed cooks: Butterfly lamb for quick grilling." By Bill Daley, August 4, 2010.

Slow lemon brisket, page 182.
"When fast is slow: Slow-cooker recipe answers call for easy, hearty meal." By Donna Pierce; recipe by Nancy Hablutzel of Chicago, November 7, 2007.

Low Country boil, page 185; Old Bay butter, page 186; Shrimp and corn stock, page 186.
"On the boil: Eating with your hands is encouraged when the dinner is a Southern-style shrimp fest." By Chris LaMorte; recipe by Mark Steuer, August 3, 2014.

Michigan baked beans, page 187.
"Slow cooking: A time-tested route to baked beans." By Robin Mather Jenkins, August 30, 2006.

Green chili with chicken, page 188.
"A bowl of green—chili, that is." By Robin Mather Jenkins, September 20, 2006.

Butterscotch praline ice cream sundae, page 193.
The plain truth: Vanilla remains the No. 1 flavor of ice cream sold in the U.S. Now it's getting richer." By Renee Enna, July 10, 2002.

Hawaiian icy, page 195.
"Home on the range: Hot ice." By Leah Eskin, August 1, 2010.

Unbelievable peanut cookies, page 196.
"You're the cook: Unbelievable peanut cookies." Recipe by Mary Ann Puchalski of Elmhurst, July 3, 2002.

Poached peaches with raspberries, page 197.
"Cook's holiday: Celebrate the Fourth with an easy outdoor menu." By Pat Dailey, June 28, 1995.

Peach crisp, page 198.
"Home on the rage: Clinging to tradition." By Leah Eskin, July 25, 2010.

Dessert bruschetta, page 201.
"Party tonight! Is it that time of year already? Yes, and these make-ahead nibbles can feed the crowd and calm the host." By Kristin Eddy, William Rice, Carol Mighton Haddix, Renee Enna, Andy Badeker, Donna Pierce and Steve Dolinsky; recipe by Steve Dolinsky, November 13, 2002.

Strawberry muffins, page 203.
"Sudden passion: The pursuit of sweet, ripe strawberries ends in a brief but intense affair." By Michael Malone, May 16, 2001.

Blueberry delight, page 204.
"Taking the raw route: A new food movement gains attention with its no-cooking, fresh-from-the-garden, approach to diet." By William Rice; recipe adapted from a recipe from Karyn Calabrese, July 30, 2003.

---

photo credits

Mojito, page 8.
Photo by Tyllie Barbosa; foodstyling by Kelly McKaig. June 5, 2005.

Basic backyard lemonade, page 11.
Photo by by James F. Quinn; foodstyling by Mark Graham. August 14, 2002.

Fruit smoothie, page 12.
Photo by Bob Fila; foodstyling by Raeanne Sarazen. March 22, 2000.

Lemon balm iced tea, page 14.
Photo by by Bob Fila; foodstyling by Corrine Kozlak. August 25, 2004.

Chocolate-covered grasshopper, page 23.
Photo by Bob Fila; foodstyling by Corrine Kozlak. July 10, 2002.

Homemade limoncello, page 27.
Photo by Bob Fila. October 8, 2003.

Nevisian smile, page 29.
Photo by Charles Osgood. July 23, 2003.

Red sangria, page 30.
Photo by Bob Fila; foodstyling by Lisa Schumacher. August 23, 2006.

Amere, page 34.
Photo by Bill Hogan, October 13, 2013.

Bella Fragola, page 37.
Photo by Bill Hogan, May 8, 2011.

House G+T and Tonic syrup, pages 38–39.
Photo by Bill Hogan, June 1 2014.

Chilled white gazpacho, page 42.
Photos by Bill Hogan. July 6, 2014.

Smoked salmon mousse, page 45.
Photo by by Bob Fila; foodstyling by Corrine Kozlak. November 13, 2002.

Snappy sausage and cucumber rounds with mustard, page 46.
Photo by by Bob Fila; foodstyling by Corrine Kozlak. November 13, 2002.

Wonton chicken bites, page 49.
Photo by by Bob Fila; foodstyling by Corrine Kozlak. November 13, 2002.

Simple ceviche, pages 50 and 51.
Photos by Bill Hogan; foodstyling by Lisa Schumacher. May 5, 2010.

Olive-avocado dim sum, page 55.
Photo by by Bob Fila; foodstyling by Corrine Kozlak. July 30, 2003.

Asian summer rolls, page 56.
Photo by Photo by Bob Fila; foodstyling by Corrine Kozlak. September 1, 2004.

Cheese and rye cocktail sandwiches, page 61.
Photo by by Bob Fila; foodstyling by Corrine Kozlak. November 13, 2002.

Pecorino crisp, page 65.
Photos by Bill Hogan. October 5, 2014.

Prosciutto wrapped figs, page 66.
Photo by Bill Hogan, October 13, 2013.

Quick crab and avocado salad, page 68.
Photo by Bill Hogan; foodstyling by Lisa Schumacher.
September 15, 2010.

Empress coleslaw, page 71.
Photos by Bob Fila; foodstyling by Corrine Kozlak.
August 28, 2002.

Red, white and blue potato salad, page 74.
Photo by Bob Fila; foodstyling by Raeanne Sarazen.
July 4, 2001.

Fingerling potato salad with tarragon, page 77.
Photo by Bob Fila; foodstyling by Raeanne Sarazen.
July 4, 2001.

Potato salad Nicoise, page 78.
Photo by Bob Fila; foodstyling by Raeanne Sarazen.
July 4, 2001.

Wild rice salad with fennel and mustard dressing,
page 83.
Photo by Bob Fila. August 27, 2003.

Marshall Field's lemon pasta salad, page 86.
Photo by Bonnie Trafelet; foodstyling by Lisa
Schumacher. August 13, 2008.

Roasted vegetable salad with apple vinaigrette,
page 88.
Photo by Bob Fila; foodstyling by Corrine Kozlak.
July 9, 2003.

Summer salad with fresh citrus vinaigrette,
page 91.
Photo by Bob Fila; foodstyling by Corrine Kozlak.
July 9, 2003.

Abundant sorrel salad, page 93.
Photo by Bill Hogan; foodstyling by Joan Moravek.
August 10, 2014.

Hot or cold beef-soba noodle salad, page 101.
Photo by Mark Graham. June 2, 2004.

Summer bean salad with Sun Gold tomatoes, herbs,
smoked trout, goat cheese dressing, page 103.
Photo by Chris Cassiday. July 9, 2014. Originally
published in "The Green City Market Cookbook"
(Agate Midway, 2014).

Grilled shrimp and pineapple salad, page 104.
Photo by Photo (color): Tropical salad gains flavor
from grilled shrimp and pineapple. Photo by Bill
Hogan; foodstyling by Lisa Schumacher. May 26,
2010.

Papa Eloy's tuna salad, page 109.
Photo by Bill Hogan; foodstyling by Lisa Schumacher.
June 26, 2013.

New Nicoise salad, page 110.
Photo by Bonnie Trafelet; foodstyling by Lisa
Schumacher. June 6, 2012.

Spinach and fingerling potato salad with warm
bacon dressing, page 113.
Photo by Bob Fila; foodstyling by Corrine Kozlak.
May 15, 2002.

Chioggia beet salad, page 114.
Photo by Bill Hogan, May 9, 2010.

Beet carpaccio, page 116.
Photos by Bill Hogan. October 5, 2014.

Tuna sandwich, page 120.
Photo by Bill Hogan; foodstyling by Joan Moravek.
July 31, 2011.

Shrimp sandwiches with chili mayonnaise,
page 123.
Photo by Bill Hogan, foodstyling by Lisa Schumacher.
September 3, 2008.

Torta Americana, page 128.
Photo by Bob Fila; foodstyling by Corrine Kozlak.
September 1, 2004.

Tofu po' boy, page 130.
Photo by Bill Hogan; foodstyling by Corrine Kozlak.
August 27, 2014.

Better than BLTs, page 133.
Photo by Bob Fila; foodstyling by Corrine Kozlak.
September 1, 2004.

Medianoche, page 135.
Photo by Bob Fila; foodstyling by Corrine Kozlak.
September 1, 2004.

Baja fish tacos and Fish tacos locos, page 136.
Photo by Bob Fila; foodstyling by Corrine Kozlak.
August 31, 2011.

Creamy cabbage slaw, page 139.
Photo by Bob Fila; foodstyling by Corrine Kozlak.
August 31, 2011.

Ethiopian chicken wraps, page 141.
Photo by Bob Fila; foodstyling by Corrine Kozlak.
September 1, 2004.

**Mackerel, carrot & herb salad sandwiches,
page 142.**
Photo by Bill Hogan, February 10, 2013.

Chicken salad sandwich, page 145.
Photo by Bill Hogan, February 12, 2012.

Grilled tomato and olive pizza, page 149.
Photo by Bonnie Trafelet; foodstyling by Corrine
Kozlak. August 13, 2008.

Grilled eggplant, page 151.
Photo by Bill Hogan; foodstyling by Joan Moravek.
August 1, 2004.

Jerk chicken pinchos, page 155.
Photo by Bill Hogan; foodstyling by Joan Moravek.
June 19, 2011.

BBQ chicken, page 157.
Photo by Bill Hogan; foodstyling by Joan Moravek.
May 20, 2012.

Simple summer chicken, page 158.
Photo by Bill Hogan; foodstyling by Joan Moravek.
June 13, 2004.

Caribbean-style garlic-soaked shrimp, page 161.
Photo by Bill Hogan; foodstyling by Corrine Kozlak.
May 30, 2012.

**Grilled branzino with smoked salt and pepper, page
162.**
Photo by Bill Hogan, May 9, 2010.

**Grilled octopus salad with grapefruit balsamic
vinegar, page 165.**
Photo by Bill Hogan, March 11, 2012.

Grilled shrimp with sambal, page 166.
Photo by Bill Hogan, June 12, 2011.

Carne asada with chimichurri, page 168.
Photo by Bill Hogan; foodstyling by Corrine Kozlak.
May 30, 2012.

Chorizo burgers with queso fresco, page 170.
Photo by Bill Hogan; foodstyling by Corrine Kozlak.
May 30, 2012.

Flank steak 4 ways, pages 146 and 175.
Photo by Bill Hogan; foodstyling by Corrine Kozlak.
May 28, 2014.

**Crying tiger flank steak marinade with sweet-hot
Thai relish, page 176.**
Photo by Bill Hogan; foodstyling by Corrine Kozlak.
May 28, 2014.

**Flank steak Levantine marinade with Yemeni hot
sauce, page 177.**
Photo by Bill Hogan; foodstyling by Corrine Kozlak.
May 28, 2014.

**Tuscan flank steak marinade with lemon-rosemary
sauce, page 178.**
Photo by Bill Hogan; foodstyling by Corrine Kozlak.
May 28, 2014.

**Cuban flank steak with mojo marinade and
churrasco, page 179**
Photo by Bill Hogan; foodstyling by Corrine Kozlak.
May 28, 2014.

Butterflied leg of lamb, page 180.
Photo by Bill Hogan; foodstyling by Corrine Kozlak.
August 4, 2010.

Slow lemon brisket, page 183.
Photo by Bob Fila; foodstyling by Lisa Schumacher.
November 7, 2007.

Low Country boil, page 184.
Photos by Bill Hogan. August 3, 2014.

Green chili with chicken, page 189.
Photo by Bob Fila; foodstyling by Lisa Schumacher.
September 20, 2006.

Hawaiian icy, page 190.
Photo by Bill Hogan; foodstyling by Joan Moravek.
August 1, 2010.

Butterscotch praline ice cream sundae, page 192.
Photo by Bob Fila; foodstyling by Corrine Kozlak.
July 10, 2002.

Peach crisp, page 199.
Photo by Bill Hogan; foodstyling by Joan Moravek.
July 25, 2010.

Dessert bruschetta, page 200.
Photo by by Bob Fila; foodstyling by Corrine Kozlak.
November 13, 2002.

Strawberry muffins, page 202.
Photo by Bob Fila; foodstyling by Raeanne Sarazen.
May 16, 2001.

index

A

abundant sorrel salad, 92
aioli, 125, 144
amere, 35
angie johnson's pasties, 127
appetizers. *See* for starters
apricot barbecue sauce, 157
asian salad of sugar snap peas, mushrooms and
 cilantro leaves, 96
asian summer rolls, 57
asparagus salad with red onion, tomato and basil, 94
avocado salsa, 171

B

bacon cooking tips, 113
bacon, turkey and beef burgers, 172
baja fish tacos, 137
baked potato salad, 73
barbecue sauce, 157
basic backyard lemonade, 10
batida, 19
BBQ chicken, 156
beef
 angie johnson's pasties, 127
 bacon, turkey and beef burgers, 172
 carne asada with chimichurri, 169
 flank steak 4 ways, 173
 hot or cold beef-soba noodle salad, 100
 mixed greens with marinated flank steak and
  herb vinaigrette, 98
 slow lemon brisket, 182
beet carpaccio, 117
bella fragola, 36
better than BLTs, 132
beverages. *See* summer quenchers
blueberry delight, 204
butterflied leg of lamb, 181
butterscotch praline ice cream sundae, 193

C

cachaca
 batida, 19
 caipirinha, 16

caipirinha, 16
caribbean-style garlic-soaked shrimp, 160
carne asada with chimichurri, 169
cauliflower and red pepper salad with sweet mustard
 dressing, 95
cheese and rye cocktail sandwiches, 61
chicken
 BBQ, 156
 ethiopian, wraps, 140
 green chili, 188
 jerk, pinchos, 154
 salad sandwich, 144
 simple summer, 159
 wonton, bites, 48
chilled white gazpacho, 63
chioggia beet salad, 115
chocolate-covered grasshopper, 22
chorizo burgers with queso fresco, 171
cocktails. *See* summer quenchers: alcoholic
coleslaw, 70, 72, 106, 138
cool treats, 191
 blueberry delight, 204
 butterscotch praline ice cream sundae, 193
 dessert bruschetta, 201
 hawaiian icy, 195
 peach crisp, 198
 poached peaches with raspberries, 197
 strawberry muffins, 203
 unbelievable peanut cookies, 196
crab. *See* shellfish
creamy basil-onion dip, 58
crispy noodle pillow, 151
crying tiger flank steak marinade with sweet-hot thai
 relish, 176
cuban flank steak with mojo marinade and churrasco,
 179
curried sweet potato salad with golden raisins and
 toasted almonds, 80

D

daiquiri, 25
dessert bruschetta, 201
desserts. *See* cool treats

E

empress coleslaw, 70
entrees. *See* summer's best main dishes
ethiopian chicken wraps, 140

F

fingerling potato salad with tarragon, 76
fish
     baja, tacos, 137
     grilled branzino with smoked salt and pepper, 163
     mackerel, carrot & herb salad sandwiches, 143
     napa slaw with charred salmon, 106
     papa eloy's tuna salad, 108
     simple ceviche, 51
     smoked salmon mousse, 44
     tacos locos, 153
     tuna sandwich, 124
flank steak 4 ways, 173
flank steak levantine marinade with yemeni hot sauce, 177
for starters, 43
     asian summer rolls, 57
     cheese and rye cocktail sandwiches, 61
     chilled white gazpacho, 63
     creamy basil-onion dip, 58
     mexican pinwheels, 62
     nut stuffing for vegetables, 52
     olive-avocado dim sum, 54
     pecorino crisp, 64
     prosciutto wrapped figs, 67
     shrimp on pesto rounds, 53
     simple ceviche, 51
     smoked salmon mousse, 44
     snappy sausage and cucumber rounds with mustard, 47
     vegetable-stuffed deviled eggs, 60
     wonton chicken bites, 48
fruit smoothie, 13

G

gin
     bella fragola, 36
     house G+T, 40
green chili with chicken, 188
grilled
     branzino with smoked salt and pepper, 163
     eggplant, 150
     english cheddar sandwich with smoked bacon and apple, 126
     octopus salad with grapefruit balsamic vinegar, 164
     shrimp and pineapple salad, 105
     shrimp with sambal, 167
     tomato and olive pizza, 148
     veggies, 152

H

handfuls, 121
     angie johnson's pasties, 127
     baja fish tacos, 137
     better than BLTs, 132
     chicken salad sandwich, 144
     ethiopian chicken wraps, 140
     grilled english cheddar sandwich with smoked bacon and apple, 126
     mackerel, carrot & herb salad sandwiches, 143
     medianoche, 134
     shrimp sandwiches with chili mayonnaise, 122
     tofu po' boy, 131
     torta americana, 129
     tuna sandwich, 124
hawaiian icy, 195
herb aioli, 144
herb-flavored simple syrups, 15
homemade limoncello, 26
hot or cold beef-soba noodle salad, 100
house G+T, 40

I

ice cream storage tips, 194
italian slaw for a crowd, 72

J

jerk chicken pinchos, 154

L

lamb, butterflied leg, 181
le jardin des huguenots, 32
lemon balm iced tea, 15
lemonade, 10
lentil salad with lemon dressing, 81
limoncello, 26
     sorrento sunset, 28
low country boil, 185

M

mackerel, carrot & herb salad sandwiches, 143
mambo, the, 20
mango, plum and peach sangria, 33
marinade, steak, 176–79
marshall field's lemon pasta salad, 87
medianoche, 134
mexican pinwheels, 62
michigan baked beans, 187

mixed greens with marinated flank steak and herb vinaigrette, 98

mojito, 18

N

napa slaw with charred salmon, 106

nevisian smile, 29

new nicoise salad, 111

nut stuffing for vegetables, 52

O

old bay butter, 186

olive-avocado dim sum, 54

P

papa eloy's tuna salad, 108

pasta salad, 84, 87

pasta salad with shallots, herbs and tomato compote, 84

peach crisp, 198

pecorino crisp, 64

pisco sour, 21

pizza, 148

poached peaches with raspberries, 197

potato salad, 73, 75, 76, 79, 80, 112

potato salad nicoise, 79

prosciutto wrapped figs, 67

Q

quick crab and avocado salad, 99

quickie aioli, 125

R

raspberry-lemon slam, 24

red sangria, 31

red, white and blue potato salad, 75

refreshing eats, 69

    abundant sorrel salad, 92

    asian salad of sugar snap peas, mushrooms and cilantro leaves, 96

    asparagus salad with red onion, tomato and basil, 94

    baked potato salad, 73

    beet carpaccio, 117

    cauliflower and red pepper salad with sweet mustard dressing, 95

    chioggia beet salad, 115

    curried sweet potato salad with golden raisins and toasted almonds, 80

    empress coleslaw, 70

    fingerling potato salad with tarragon, 76

    grilled shrimp and pineapple salad, 105

    hot or cold beef-soba noodle salad, 100

    italian slaw for a crowd, 72

    lentil salad with lemon dressing, 81

    marshall field's lemon pasta salad, 87

    mixed greens with marinated flank steak and herb vinaigrette, 98

    napa slaw with charred salmon, 106

    new nicoise salad, 111

    papa eloy's tuna salad, 108

    pasta salad with shallots, herbs and tomato compote, 84

    potato salad nicoise, 79

    quick crab and avocado salad, 99

    red, white and blue potato salad, 75

    roasted pepper and onion salad with goat cheese and orange, 85

    roasted vegetable salad with apple vinaigrette, 89

    seared scallops with a fennel olive and red onion salad, 107

    spinach and fingerling potato salad with warm bacon dressing, 112

    summer bean salad with sun gold tomatoes, herbs, smoked trout, goat cheese dressing, 102

    summer salad with fresh citrus vinaigrette, 90

    swiss cheese salad, 97

    wild rice salad with fennel and mustard dressing, 82

roasted pepper and onion salad with goat cheese and orange, 85

roasted vegetable salad with apple vinaigrette, 89

rum

    daiquiri, 25

    mambo, the, 20

    mango, plum and peach sangria, 33

    mojito, 18

    nevisian smile, 29

S

salads. *See* refreshing eats

salsa fresca, 138

salsa verde, 155

sandwiches. *See* handfuls

sangria

    le jardin des huguenots, 32

    mango, plum and peach sangria, 33

    red sangria, 31

seared scallops with a fennel olive and red onion salad, 107

shellfish

    caribbean-style garlic-soaked shrimp, 160

    grilled shrimp and pineapple salad, 105

    grilled shrimp with sambal, 167

    low country boil, 185

quick crab and avocado salad, 99
seared scallops with a fennel, olive and red onion salad, 107
shrimp on pesto rounds, 53
shrimp sandwiches with chili mayonnaise, 122
shrimp. *See also* shellfish
corn stock, and, 186
pesto rounds, 53
sandwiches with chili mayonnaise, 122
simple
ceviche, 51
summer chicken, 159
syrup, 17
herb-flavored, 15
slow lemon brisket, 182
smoked salmon mousse, 44
smoothie, 13
snappy sausage and cucumber rounds with mustard, 47
sorrento sunset, 28
spinach and fingerling potato salad with warm bacon dressing, 112
strawberry muffins, 203
summer bean salad with sun gold tomatoes, herbs, smoked trout, goat cheese dressing, 102
summer quenchers, 9
alcoholic
amere, 35
batida, 19
bella fragola, 36
caipirinha, 16
chocolate-covered grasshopper, 22
daiquiri, 25
homemade limoncello, 26
house G+T, 40
le jardin des huguenots, 32
mambo, the, 20
mango, plum and peach sangria, 33
mojito, 18
nevisian smile, 29
pisco sour, 21
raspberry-lemon slam, 24
red sangria, 31
sorrento sunset, 28
nonalcoholic
basic backyard lemonade, 10
fruit smoothie, 13
lemon balm iced tea, 15
summer salad with fresh citrus vinaigrette, 90

summer's best main dishes, 147
bacon, turkey and beef burgers, 172
BBQ chicken, 156
butterflied leg of lamb, 181
caribbean-style garlic-soaked shrimp, 160
carne asada with chimichurri, 169
chorizo burgers with queso fresco, 171
fish tacos locos, 153
flank steak 4 ways, 173
green chili with chicken, 188
grilled
branzino with smoked salt and pepper, 163
eggplant, 150
octopus salad with grapefruit balsamic vinegar, 164
shrimp with sambal, 167
tomato and olive pizza, 148
veggies, 152
jerk chicken pinchos, 154
low country boil, 185
michigan baked beans, 187
simple summer chicken, 159
slow lemon brisket, 182
swiss cheese salad, 97

T
tequila
raspberry-lemon slam, 24
tofu po' boy, 131
tonic syrup, 41
torta americana, 129
tuna sandwich, 124
tuscan flank steak marinade with lemon-rosemary sauce, 178

U
unbelievable peanut cookies, 196

V
vegetable-stuffed deviled eggs, 60
vodka
homemade limoncello, 26
mango, plum and peach sangria, 33

W
whiskey
amere, 35
wild rice salad with fennel and mustard dressing, 82
wonton chicken bites, 48